Essential Perl 5 for
Web Professionals

ISBN 0-13-012653-5

90000

9 780130 126535

Other Books in the Series

- *Essential CSS & DHTML for Web Professionals*
  Dan Livingston and Micah Brown

- *Essential Photoshop 5 for Web Professionals*
  Brad Eigen, Dan Livingston, and Micah Brown

- *Essential JavaScript for Web Professionals*
  Dan Barrett, Dan Livingston, and Micah Brown

Essential Perl 5 for Web Professionals

Micah Brown
Etail Enterprises

Chris Bellew

Dan Livingston
Wire Man Productions

Prentice Hall PTR
Upper Saddle River, NJ 07458
http://www.phptr.com

Library of Congress Cataloging-in-Publication Data

Brown, Micah.
  Essential Perl 5 for Web professionals / Micah Brown, Chris Bellew,
Dan Livingston.
      p. cm -- (Prentice Hall essential Web professionals series)
    ISBN 0-13-012653-5(pbk.)
    1. Perl (Computer program language) I. Bellew, Chris. II. Livingston, Dan.
  III. Title. IV. Series.
  QA76.73.P22B77   1999
  005.13'3--dc21   99-32974
                                                                       CIP

Editorial/Production Supervision: Benchmark Productions, Inc.
Acquisitions Editor: Karen McLean
Cover Design Director: Jerry Votta
Cover Design: Scott Weiss
Cover Illustration: Jean Francois Podevin, from *The Stock Illustration Source, Vol. 5.*
Manufacturing Manager: Alexis R. Heydt
Editorial Assistant: Audri Anna Bazlen
Marketing Manager: Dan Rush
Project Coordinator: Anne Trowbridge

© 1999 Prentice Hall PTR
Prentice-Hall, Inc.
Upper Saddle River, NJ 07458

Prentice Hall books are widely used by corporations and government agencies for
training, marketing, and resale.

The publisher offers discounts on this book when ordered in bulk quantities.
For more information, contact: Corporate Sales Department, Phone: 800-382-3419;
Fax: 201-236-7141; E-mail: corpsales@prenhall.com; or write: Prentice Hall P T R,
Corp. Sales Dept., One Lake Street, Upper Saddle River, NJ 07458.

Printed in the United States of America

10 9 8 7 6 5 4 3 2 1

ISBN 0-13-012653-5

Prentice-Hall International (UK) Limited, *London*
Prentice-Hall of Australia Pty. Limited, *Sydney*
Prentice-Hall Canada Inc., *Toronto*
Prentice-Hall Hispanoamericana, S.A., *Mexico*
Prentice-Hall of India Private Limited, *New Delhi*
Prentice-Hall of Japan, Inc., *Tokyo*
Prentice-Hall (Singapore) Pte. Ltd., *Singapore*
Editora Prentice-Hall do Brasil, Ltda., *Rio de Janeiro*

Contents

Introduction

To stay competitive on the Internet it is important for Web developers to be able to create sites that allow interaction with users. Perl can help you do that! Perl was one of the first languages written for programming on the World Wide Web, and to this day still, it remains one of the most popular.

When we first delved into Perl programming, we were not able to locate any manuals that could teach us Perl in a quick and concise manner. Our only options were to either purchase a 4" thick manual that would take weeks to sort through (and could easily double as a doorstop), or purchase instructional material that was too "techie" for our taste.

This book is different in that it allows you to start programming immediately and see actual results while learning the Perl language. In this book you will find some of the most commonly used Perl scripts that will allow your site to interact with your users. Our instructions utilize a simple step by step approach that explains what is happening and why.

◆ How This Book Is Laid Out

In the first three chapters you will learn how to set up interactive scripts for Shelley Biotechnologies, a fast-growing biotech startup. Each chapter contains at least one sub-project that consists of commonly used Perl scripts that range from beginner to intermediate levels. At the end of each chapter there will be advanced exercises that will help to expand your skills.

In the second half of the book you will work with some more advanced programs for *Stitch Magazine*'s Web site. These examples are more advanced than those found in the first project, and will show you some of the powerful things you can do with Perl.

All of the examples in the book will be located on the companion Web site at http://www.phptr.com/essential. You will be able to download the HTML and scripts needed to follow along with the exercises.

◆ The Origin of Perl

Perl was brought to life in 1987 when Larry Wall created it as a tool to aid in his system administration tasks. Perl officially stands for "Practical Extraction Report Language," but some refer to it as "Pathologically Eclectic Rubbish Lister." In any case, it is a very flexible and powerful language that can handle many tasks, from system administration to controlling input and output with users on your Web pages.

Perl was originally written to handle the tasks of reading data from files, manipulating data, and writing reports on the data. However, over the years, and through several developments, Perl has been adopted into the Web community as one of the most widely used languages to write CGI (Common Gateway Interface) applications to produce more sophisticated and interactive pages for Web sites. Perl can handle the tasks of writing simple text to your Web pages, or gathering information from a customer and e-mailing it back to you. It can handle more complex tasks such as reading and writing to a database file to keep track of your company's inventory, or even writing customer information you just received via e-mail into a customer contact database. The possibilities are endless.

For all of you eggheads out there who want to be a little more informed on the inner workings of Perl, it is basically a crossbreed of sed, awk, sh, and the C languages.

Unlike C, it is an interpreted language in that it does not need to be compiled into a machine-only readable file first in order to run. It runs as a standard text application that you may go in and edit freely and easily without all the hassles of compiling and recompiling every time you wish to make a change. This makes it very nice and much quicker in the long run.

Currently (as of this writing) Perl is at version 5.005. Perl was originally written for Unix, but during the years it has been ported over to several other operating systems such as Windows 95, Windows NT, OS/2, Macintosh, BeOS, and even Amiga, among many others.

You can find the latest release of Perl in various places on the Internet, including a link from http://www.phptr.com/essential, which is also the Web site companion for this book.

◆ Is Your System Able to Run Perl?

A good question to ask yourself before starting something like programming with Perl is whether or not you actually have the means to use the program on your particular system. For the majority of our exercises, we will assume you are using Perl on a Unix-type machine. Later in this book we will also look at running Perl on a Windows-type machine, but for now we will only be using Unix in order to be consistent and because this is the most widely used OS for this type of situation. If you are running Perl on a Windows machine, just so you know up front, there really isn't a whole lot of difference between the two—just a few minor changes here and there.

In order to successfully use this book, you should make sure that your Internet Service Provider (ISP):

- Is currently using Perl 5
- Has a telnet session directly to the machine that's running Perl 5
- Will allow you to write your own scripts

If you are not sure if your ISP machine is running Perl, you should call your ISP or check its homepage to see whether or not these services are provided with your account.

If your ISP does not offer these services or you currently do not have a provider, then you should find one that does. We suggest you check out Hurricane Electric Internet Services (www.he.net). We've always had really good service with them and they have one of the lowest prices on the Net that we've come across.

For the purpose of this book, we are assuming that you already have a fundamental background in HTML. It is also helpful if you have a basic knowledge of how a programming language works. While it is not totally necessary for you to already have these skills, because we will be taking you through the exercises step by step, it will make the learning process easier if you already know the basics.

◆ What Version of Perl Are You Running?

There are several different types of platforms you can use to run Perl. Throughout this book we will be showing you examples of these scripts running from a Unix-type machine.

NOTE

When we mention *command line*, we are referring to a telnet session that is running from our machine to the Unix server and working in a shell environment. It will typically appear as shown in Figure I-1.

If you are using Windows as your environment, then the command line will be your DOS prompt.

First off, you will need to get a telnet session going with the machine on which you will be doing your scripts. Once you have logged in to the machine and you have a command-line prompt, you should check to see which version of Perl you are using. This is done with the –v command:

```
perl -v
```

You should then see a window similar to the one shown in Figure I-1.

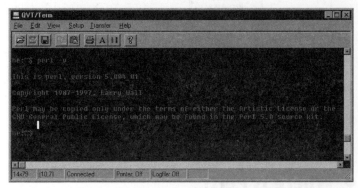

FIGURE I–1 This is what a typical telnet session will look like. Typing in `perl -v` at the command line will tell you what version of Perl is running on your system.

This tells you that Perl, version 5.004_01, is being used on this system, plus some extra copyright information that you probably don't really need to know unless you are really into this kind of stuff. Your system might be running a different version of Perl, but any 5.x version of Perl will be fine for this book.

◆ How HTML and Perl Work Together

While Perl was originally intended for use as a system administration tool, over the years people began to realize that with its flexibility, Perl was a great language to make their Web pages more interactive and dynamic for their viewers. Someone even wrote a Web server with Perl called "Plexus."

To get a visual of how CGI works with the server, take a look at Figure I-2.

When a user's Web browser goes to access a link from your Web page that is linked to your Perl script, first it accesses the HTTP server and then the Perl program. Once the Perl program interprets the script, it is then passed back to the HTTP server and then to the user. Simple enough, right?

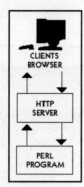

FIGURE I–2 How CGI works with the server

◆ Where Is Perl?

The first thing we need to find out is where the Perl program is located on the system on which you will be writing your scripts. This will be a line of code that will be put into the beginning of every script you write to instruct the machine to run the Perl program and execute your script. To find this, you will need to go to your command line and type in:

```
whereis perl
```

Here is an example that is common on most systems:

```
#/usr/bin/perl
```

On some systems it might be a slightly different path depending on where the system administrator stores the program. Sometimes several versions of Perl are running and more than one location will be returned from the whereis perl command. Another common location is

```
#/usr/local/bin/perl
```

Once you find where Perl is located, make a note of it because you will be referring to it quite often from here on out.

◆ Running Perl on Windows

If you are planning to run Perl on a Windows 9.x or Windows NT system you do not need to have this line in the beginning of your script as long as the Perl program is within your path. Perl does not come preloaded with these systems, so in order for you to run scripts on your Windows machines you will need to download and install it. The nicest and easiest one that we have found is a program called "Active Perl" from Active State. This program will install Perl onto your Windows 9.x or Windows NT machine and then add Perl to your system's path for you. If you want to grab a free copy, you can find it at http://www.ActiveState.com/ActivePerl/.

◆ What Other Programs Are Used for CGI

There are several programs available to write a CGI to your Web pages, but, as we mentioned earlier, none are as widely used or quite as universal as the Perl scripting language.

Some other programs used for CGI are

- C language
- C++
- Tcl or Tk
- PHP
- Unix Shell sh, ksh, csh
- Visual Basic
- ASP
- AppleScript

◆ Notes About This Book and the Web Site

http://www.phptr.com/essential

All the code throughout the book is available on the book's Web site. It is suggested that you attempt to write as much of it yourself as you can in order to get used to all the different commands Perl has to offer. Through the process of doing this, you will encounter some mistakes due to typos you will undoubtedly make (if you don't, then we owe you a Coke), but this is the best way to learn because you must go back and study what could have gone wrong. We have found that the best way to learn is by doing it.

All the HTML that is used in the examples throughout the book is located on the Web site as well, plus the answers to all of the "Advanced Projects" at the end of each chapter. We encourage you to play around with these to further develop your skills as a Perl programmer.

There are also three appendices in case you need further explanation of the functions in this book. Appendix A, "An Introduction to Forms," is a tutorial on how HTML forms work, and all the different types you can use to gather different types of information through your form pages. Appendix B, "Stepping through the Perly Gates," is a tutorial on Perl. While it is not by any means a complete tutorial, it will definitely get you well acquainted with the language. Appendix C, "Miscellaneous Reference," is a reference for some of the most typical mistakes you might encounter when writing a Perl script. There is also a list of places that you can check out to further your studies with Perl.

In this *Essential Web Professionals* series, we have created two fictitious companies that we feel portray a large percentage of the types of companies that are getting involved with exposure on the Web.

- *Stitch Magazine: Stitch* is an online fashion magazine that has chosen to publish parts of the magazine on the Web to complement its printed version. It's also using the Web to reach new readers.
- Shelley Biotechnologies: This is a company that sells biotech products and wishes to enter the online world to advertise them.

Although every company is different in its own way, we have found that most really do fall into one of these two categories.

◆ What This Book Will and Won't Teach You

Perl can be a very complex language depending on how deeply you want to get into it to do some rather complex problem solving. We won't be going into the complete language in this book—just what you need to learn to start programming for the Web. We have taken some of the most widely used types of scripts that you will encounter as a Web developer, and put them together in an easy-to-read, step by step approach. The appendices at the back of the book give you a quick rundown on how to use forms, how to build the front end of your site, and a great tutorial on the Perl language and the various parts of it you will be learning in this book to build the back end.

By the end of this book you will be able to take these scripts and modify them to your heart's content to build your own interactive applications to use for your personal or corporate Web site.

If you're a complete rookie and just starting out in the wonderful world of programming, or maybe you have a little experience but need to brush up, then you should first look through the appendices. Otherwise, if you think you have a handle on all the information they contain and just want to jump into learning some Perl scripting, then by all means, JUMP!

Acknowledgments

◆ Micah Brown

I would like to give special thanks to my wife, Dawn, who has helped me in too many ways to mention. You are my love, my life, and most importantly, my best friend. I dedicate this book to her and our daughter, Ashley Nova, who has yet to be born into this world—we can't wait to meet you!

Also, a special thanks to my parents, William and Donna, and my extended parents, Beppe and Joy, for everything they have done for me these last 29 years. I wouldn't be the person I am today if it weren't for them. I will always be grateful for how much you all have taught me through the years and helped me to grow as a person.

Thanks to Mark Taub and Karen McLean for helping Dan and me get this book series out of our brains and onto paper. You are right, this is a little tougher than we had first imagined! Also, thanks to Carl Gorman, my partner in crime at Etail Enterprises (www.etail.com), and my band members, Kelly and Carl from Nitrus, for putting up with me through all of this.

Finally, thanks to my co-authors, Chris Bellew and Dan Livingston, as well as all the others who worked on the books in this series. If it weren't for you, I wouldn't be writing this.

◆ Chris Bellew

I would like to thank my parents for all their support in everything I do. A big thanks to my brother Mike for being someone I could look up to all my life. I'd also like to thank my friends, Derek, Kelly, Carl, Brad, and Dan, for the fun times that make working tolerable.

A special thanks to April for being such a cool person, and of course my co-authors, Micah and Dan, for getting me in on this project. Also, thanks to everyone at Prentice Hall.

Lastly, thanks to the authors of the Camel books, without whom I probably wouldn't know Perl as well as I do (definitely recommended).

◆ Dan Livingston

We had the good luck to work with Mark Taub and Karen McLean from Prentice Hall on this project. We especially tested Karen's cattle-herding skills, and she remained remarkably patient and focused throughout the process.

I would like to thank my fiancée, Tanya Muller, for her continuing patience and encouragement. I wouldn't have been able to write this book while starting my own business without her by my side. Her support was, and continues to be, invaluable.

I'd also like to thank W. Bradley Scott of Clear Ink for coming up with the idea of using an online fashion magazine as a fictional company. He also acted as technical reviewer, and was generally very helpful.

Finally, I'd like to thank my design mentor, Brad Eigen of MadBoy Productions. He's the Daddy.

About the Authors

◆ Micah Brown

After working in the print industry for several years, Micah Brown started his career with the Web industry back in 1995 as both a programmer and designer. Some of the sites Micah has under his belt are Dr. Laura, Pacific Bell, Amazing Discoveries, and Ascend Communications.

Micah has also been a technical reviewer for Prentice Hall for the last three years for various publications, most notably *Perl by Example* by Ellie Quigley.

Micah is currently a co-owner of Etail Enterprises, a Web consulting firm located in southern California that specializes in bringing companies into this new arena of online advertising.

◆ Chris Bellew

With over seven years of experience in the computer industry and studying at Northern Arizona University, Chris specializes in languages such as Perl, ASP, Tango, and PHP. His clientele includes Hewlett-Packard, MacSys, and Pacific Bell.

◆ Dan Livingston

Coming from a background in marine biology, Dan Livingston was drawn to Web design in early 1996. His Web sites have since included high-profile clients such as Apple, Pacific Bell, and Novell. His sites have won numerous awards, and have been featured both in design books and on *CNN Prime Time*. His envelope-pushing DHTML site, Palette Man, has received international recognition, as well as "Cool Site" awards from Yahoo!, Macromedia, and *USA Today*. Dan was a Web designer and scripter at the Web design firm Clear Ink before starting his own successful design/user interface company, Wire Man Productions. He continues to produce titles for Prentice Hall's *Essential* series.

1 Learning to Read and Write

c h a p t e r

IN THIS CHAPTER

- New Features
- Reading External Files with Perl
- Reading an External File through a Browser
- Project I: Automating Articles
- Project II: Writing to External Files
- Recap
- Advanced Projects

Let's say you walk into work one Monday morning ready to continue your work as a page layout designer for the upscale Stitch Magazine. *As you take your first sip of coffee your phone rings and it's the president of the company on the other line. He starts rambling on and on about some brainstorm that he and the upper management team had over the weekend about taking the magazine and putting it up on the Web for millions to see!*

You start to tell him, "Uh sir, are you sure you dialed the right extension? I really don't know how to do that." So, of course, he tells you to figure it out. How hard can it be? For the rest of the week you study the wonderful and challenging world of HTML and page layout design with such books as Essential Photoshop 5 for Web Professionals, *and learn the intricacies of setting up a Web site for* Stitch.

After you've spent a couple of weeks learning HTML and designing an online version of your company's magazine, you have a pretty nice-looking site and

*decide to call your boss and brag about it. When he gets back to you he says,
"Great, great! But we need more! We need to have a user response form, a
message board, a place where people can vote on questions posed in articles,
search engines, monkeys flying across the screen and juggling the images
around." You tell him you'll jump right on it, knowing that bonuses are just
around the corner.*

Being one of those brilliant people, you pick up this book, Essential Perl 5
for Web Professionals, *and thumb through it. This book will teach you
how to do everything your boss wants you to do to the company's site and
more (with the exception of his reference to monkeys, but you think you'll
figure out what the heck he was talking about later).*

*To start this chapter off, you're going to have to learn a few functions. After you
learn some of these you will be able to work with the scripts that follow.*

◆ New Features

print

print is used for exactly what it says, to print information to
STDOUT (standard output) or an alternate output. This can be
what is printed to the screen, a file, or another program.

Variables

With Perl there are only three types of variables, unlike other
languages, which may have many types.

- Scalar
- Array
- Associative array

A scalar is a single value that is assigned information,
whether it be an integer or a sentence. A scalar variable starts
with a $ to distinguish itself from the other types of variables
such as the array, which uses a @, or the associative array,
which uses a %.

Syntax

```
$someValue = 5;
$someName = "This sentence is assigned to the
variable to the left";
```

Quotes

There are two types of quotes you will be dealing with: single
(' ') and double (" ").

Single quotes

These are very literal quotes. If you would like to print out a variable and you put it between single quotes, the actual variable name will be printed instead of the actual value.

```
print 'I'm thinking of the number: $number';
```
***Result:* I'm thinking of the number: $number**

What you see between the single quotes is what you get—WYSIWYG.

Double quotes

Double quotes are a little friendlier than the single quotes in that they aren't quite as literal. If the scalar variable `$number` were assigned the value 5, here's what the result would look like:

Syntax

```
print "I'm thinking of the number: $number";
```
***Result:* I'm thinking of the number: 5**

Double quotes will also allow you to use special characters like the newline character \n to start a new line, whereas single quotes will actually just print \n.

NOTE
You probably noticed the semicolon (;) at the end of some of these lines. This is to let Perl know that the end of that statement has been reached and it's time to start a new one.

open

The `open` function allows you to open a file to read, write, or append to. You can also use this function to open a process such as sendmail through a pipe (|), which you will get a look at in the next chapter.

Syntax

Opening a file:
```
open(FILEHANDLE, "FILENAME") ;
```

Opening a process:
```
open(FILEHANDLE, "|/usr/sbin/sendmail");
```

FILEHANDLES

FILEHANDLES are used as unique identifiers, or labels, when accessing other files when opening, closing, editing, or doing anything with those files. Their names usually appear in upper-case letters; this is not necessary, as they will work in lowercase as well. As a proper rule, however, you should use uppercase.

Syntax

```
open(ARTICLE1, ">article1.txt");
```

When referring to article1.txt you will use the `ARTICLE1` as the FILEHANDLE.

Syntax

```
print ARTICLE1 "this will be added to article1.txt";
```

NOTE

You can give FILEHANDLEs any name you wish, other than those used by the Perl language.

---

close

Whenever you open a file or a process, it is usually good practice to `close` it when you are finished using it. This is not required, but not doing so could produce some problems.

Syntax

Closing a file:
```
open(FILEHANDLE, "FILENAME") ;
close(FILEHANDLE);
```

Closing a process:
```
open(FILEHANDLE, "|/usr/sbin/sendmail");
close(FILEHANDLE);
```

while

With the `while` statement, we take a variable that has earlier been assigned a value and test it to see whether it is true or not. This is called the *condition*. If the condition of the variable is true, then the statement will be executed. If the condition of the variable is false, then the statement after the `while` will be ignored and we move on to the next part of the code.

Syntax

```
while(condition)
{
    ( statements );
}
```

The special $_ variable

Perl has a special variable for use in many different operations, such as the current line of a loop that is reading the contents of a FILEHANDLE, or a number of regular expression matches. In the case of a loop (while, foreach, and so forth), Perl automatically copies the current line being read into $_. This can save a lot of typing when using other operations when one or more parameters are $_. You will learn how we use $_ in the many examples in this book.

Escape Sequences

These are sequences of characters that consist of a backslash (\) followed by one or more characters that perform certain duties, as shown in Table 1–1. The most common one you will see is \n, which formats a new line. When you use the backslash, the character that follows it performs some action. If you want to actually print the character \, then you simply throw a \ in front of that: \\.

TABLE 1–1 Escape Sequences

Escape Sequence	Description
\a	Bell or a beep
\b	Backspace
\e	Escape
\f	Form feed
\l	Force the next character into lowercase
\L	Force all following characters into lowercase
\n	Newline
\r	Carriage return
\t	Tab
\u	Force the next character into uppercase
\U	Force all following characters into uppercase
\v	Vertical tab

◆ Reading External Files with Perl

Script 1–1 is a simple script that allows you to open an ordinary text file and print it to the screen. To begin, start with this simple text file, which we will use for the next couple of examples. Name the file article1.txt and write the following lines as its contents:

article1.txt

Self protection
How to fend off an attacker with your stiletto heel.

To open a file for reading, use the open command. Makes sense, right? Then you need to assign a FILEHANDLE to it and the name of the file you wish to open.

Script 1–1
read.cgi

```
#!/usr/bin/perl
open(ARTICLE1, "article1.txt");
while (<ARTICLE1>) # like while($_ = <ARTICLE1>)
{
    print; # like print($_);
}
close (ARTICLE1);
```

When run from the command line, this script prints out the contents of article1.txt, which is what we want. First, what this does is open article1.txt and assign it the FILEHANDLE ARTICLE1. The while statement takes the ARTICLE1 FILEHAN-DLE so that *while* this file still has content, it gets printed. Then the FILEHANDLE ARTICLE1 is closed.

Once you have both article1.txt and read.cgi saved, go to a command prompt in that directory and type:

```
perl read.cgi
```

The contents of article1.txt will be output to your screen just as expected.

This is great and all, but you want to publish these .txt files as Web pages. If you try to load Script 1–1 from your browser, you'll get an error. In order to avoid an error, an HTML Content-type needs to be defined, and the appropriate HTML header and footer information needs to be set to format the HTML page.

Whenever you write a script that will output anything to the browser, you need to use a `Content-type` to let the script and the browser know how to communicate with each other. After you open a `Content-type` you can then use the `print` command to print HTML tags to format your output to the browser.

◆ Reading an External File through a Browser

Script 1–2 shows you a simple way to have your script print out an external file through your browser.

Script 1–2
readarticle.cgi

```
     #!/usr/bin/perl
1.   print "Content-type: text/html\n\n";
2.   print "<HTML>\n<BODY BGCOLOR=\"#FFFFFF\">\n\n";

3.   open(ARTICLE1, "article1.txt");
4.   while (<ARTICLE1>)
5.   {
6.       print;
7.   }
8.   close (ARTICLE1);
9.   print "</BODY>\n";
10.  print "</HTML>";
```

HOW THE SCRIPT WORKS

1. This line tells the browser to expect HTML during this function. If this is not included, the browser has no way of knowing that this is HTML content and things will undoubtedly get a little screwy.

2. This next line is where the script starts writing the HTML tags with the header tags. Be sure to watch out for special characters that do not print correctly (such as quotes) and precede them with a backslash (`\`). Follow all the remaining HTML code like this in a similar manner.

3. The script is now told to `open` article1.txt and assign the name `ARTICLE1` as the FILEHANDLE.

4–7. Open the `ARTICLE` FILEHANDLE and loop through each line. During each iteration of the loop, the contents of the

current line are stored in $_. Using `print` with no argu-
ments simply prints out $_, the current line of the file.

8. Close the FILEHANDLE.

9-10. Now you need to close off the file with the footer HTML
tags followed by the \n (line break) tags to make the format look nice and clean.

NOTE

These are simple .txt files and will not print out line breaks unless they
are coded with HTML tags in the .txt file.

◆ Project I: Automating Articles

Throughout the projects in this book, we will list the files you will
be using along with the permissions you will need to issue these
files. For a description of how to change permissions on your files
in Unix, please check out the brief tutorial on file permissions
toward the end of Appendix B, "Miscellaneous Reference."

Files Used	Permissions
article1.html	644
article2.html	644
article3.html	644
random.cgi	755
readme.cgi	755

Now let's see how to go about automating your articles with
simple Perl scripts. Since you already have the header and footer
information in the script, you can build your article HTML files
without them. Otherwise, you will end up with duplicate header
and footer tags.

Use the following three HTML files with their appropriate filenames (we will use these in the next few projects):

article1.html

```
<TITLE>Article 1</TITLE>
<FONT SIZE="4"><B>Self protection</B></FONT><P>
<FONT SIZE="3">How to fend off an attacker with your
stiletto heel.</FONT>
```

article2.html

```
<TITLE>Article 2</TITLE>
<FONT SIZE="4"><B>Salads!!!</B></FONT><P>
<FONT SIZE="3">1001 ways to make salads.</FONT>
```

article3.html

```
<TITLE>Article 3</TITLE>
<FONT SIZE="4"><B>Micro Minis are back</B></FONT><P>
<FONT SIZE="3">Just how short is too short?</FONT>
```

Randomize

For our first project with the three HTML files you have just created, you will use the script random.cgi that will randomly display one of these files every time a user visits your Web page.
Here is your first look at an array that is used to store the names
of the files that will be randomly picked to be displayed. This is
done by using the `srand` and `rand` functions.

NEW FEATURES

array

An array is another type of variable, but instead of holding a
single piece of data, an array can hold several. A scalar variable begins with a $, whereas an array begins with a @. (An
easy way to remember an array is by the a in the @ sign.) An
array sorts these different fields by indexing them in order
starting with 0. Note that it does not begin with 1 as you
would think it would.

Syntax

```
name = ("Micah", "Chris", "Dan");
print "Array field 0 is: $name[0]\n";
print "Array field 1 is: $name[1]\n";
print "Array field 2 is: $name[2]\n";
```

Results

```
Array field 0 is: Micah
Array field 1 is: Chris
Array field 2 is: Dan
```

srand

The srand function initializes the random-number generator.

rand

The rand function takes as its argument an integer and then generates a random number between 0 and the integer.

Script 1–3
random.cgi

```
#!/usr/bin/perl
print "Content-type: text/html\n\n";
print "<HTML>\n<BODY BGCOLOR=\"#FFFFFF\">\n\n";
1.  srand;
2.  @articles = ("article1.html", "article2.html",
                "article3.html");
3.  $random_number = rand(@articles);
4.  $article = $articles[$random_number];
5.  open(FILE, $article);
6.  while(<FILE>)
    {
7.      print $_;
    }
    close(FILE);
    print "</BODY>\n";
    print "</HTML>\n";
```

HOW THE SCRIPT WORKS

1. The srand function initializes the random-number generator.

2. Now an array called @articles is created, and the three files article1.html, article2.html, and article3.html are added to it. If you would like to use more than these three files or other filenames, you can simply add them in place of these. You can have as many files as you wish.

3. This is where the rand function comes into play. The rand function takes as its argument an integer, which then generates a random number between 0 and the integer. This way, a random index is chosen from the @articles array. The value is then assigned to the variable $random_number.

4. Next, we assign the chosen filename associated with the index that was randomly selected from the @articles array and place it in a new variable called $article.

```
$article = $articles[$random_number];
```

5. open(FILE, $article); The file $article is now opened and assigned the FILEHANDLE FILE.

6–7. Now the script loops through all the lines of the file line by line while the FILE FILEHANDLE is open. While this is looping through the FILEHANDLE, during each iteration of the loop the current line of the FILEHANDLE is assigned to the special $_ variable (including the carriage return at the end). Simply printing out this variable is all that is needed. Through each iteration of the file, each line is printed out. This is the same thing that is done by the cat command in Unix, or the type command in MS-DOS/Windows.

Displaying Files by Time of Day

What if you want to display one of the three articles based on the time of day? For example, article1 from 12:01 A.M. to 8 A.M., article2 from 8:01 A.M. to 4 P.M., and article3 from 4:01 P.M. to midnight. This script will show you how by taking the $hour variable from a function called localtime, and then testing the variable with a series of if statements to determine which file to spit out to the browser.

NEW FUNCTIONS

if (statement)

The if statement tests whether a condition is true or not. If the statement is not true, it moves on.

elsif (statement)

Once the if statement has been executed, the elsif function is used to test if another condition is true.

else (statement)

else is used at the end of an if block statement to handle anything that wasn't in the previous conditions—kind of like a catch-all statement.

You can use the if statement with several elsif statements, but only use the else statement one time, which will be at the end of the entire block of if statements. See Table 1–2 for some examples of how to and how not to use these statements.

TABLE 1–2 Uses of the Else Statements

Good	Bad!
`if`	`if`
(statement);	(statement);
`elsif`	`else`
(statement);	(statement);
`elsif`	`else`
(statement);	(statement);
`else`	`else`
(statement);	(statement);

localtime

The `localtime` function returns an array of nine elements of time in the following order:

```
($sec,$min,$hour,$mday,$mon,$year,$wday,$yday,$isdst) =
localtime(time);
```

TABLE 1–3

Array Number	Value
0	Seconds
1	Minutes
2	Hour of the day (0–23)
3	Day of the month
4	Month (0 = January, 11 = December)
5	Year (with 1900 subtracted from it)
6	Day of the week (0 = Sunday, 6 = Saturday)
7	Day of the year (0–364)
8	A flag indicating whether it is daylight savings time

Script 1–4
readme.cgi

```
#!/usr/bin/perl
print "Content-type: text/html\n\n";
```
1.
```
($sec,$min,$hour,$mday,$mon,$year,$wday,$yday,$isdst) =
localtime(time);
```

```
2.  if(($hour >= 0) && ($hour < 9))
    {
        $article = "article1.html";
    }
3.  elsif(($hour > 8) && ($hour < 16))
    {
        $article = "article2.html ";
    }
4.  else
    {
        $article = "article3.html ";
    }
5.  open(FILE, $article);
6.  while(<FILE>)
    {
7.      print $_;
    }
    close (FILE);
```

HOW THE SCRIPT WORKS

1. The `localtime` function returns an array of nine elements and assigns these values to their associated variables, `$sec`, `$min`, `$hour`, `$mday`, `$mon`, `$year`, `$wday`, `$yday`, `$isdst`.

2–7. These next several lines use the `if`, `elsif`, and `else` functions to check to see if these variables meet certain criteria:

`if(($hour >= 0) && ($hour < 9))`: First, the script looks to see if the `$hour` variable is between the hours of midnight (0) and 8 A.M. (8) by seeing if it is equal to or greater than 0 and less than 9. `&&` is the logical operator used for "and." If this is true, then the variable `$article` is assigned the value article1.html. If not, then the script moves on to the next statement.

`elsif(($hour > 8) && ($hour < 16))`: Now the script checks to see if the `$hour` variable is between 8 A.M. and 4 P.M. If this is true, then the variable `$article` is assigned the value article2.html. If not, then the script moves on to the next statement.

`else`: Finally, if none of the previous tests were true, then a final test is done, which is just an `else` (in this case it is a catch-all), and `$article` is assigned the value article3.html.

◆ Project II: Writing to External Files

Files Used	Permissions
write.cgi	755
write.html	744
numbers (you'll need to create this directory)	755

In the past few scripts you learned how to open up external files and display the output to the browser. With the write.cgi script and write.html file, you will see how to use an HTML interface to enter information into three fields, then have the script write that to an individual HTML file to a specified directory. In this case, you will use a directory named `numbers`.

Once this is done, the script will then list all of the files it has written to the `numbers` directory with a hot-link to them so you may view them.

NEW FEATURES

Writing to a file

```
open(FILEHANDLE, ">file.html");
```
> will write to a file. If copy already exists in this file it will be overwritten.

```
open(FILEHANDLE, ">>file.html");
```
>> will append to the file. If content exists, the new content will be added to the end of the file, thus preserving the existing content.

opendir

```
opendir(FILEHANDLE, "directory");
```
Similar to the `open` function where you specify a FILEHANDLE for a folder instead of a file to be opened.

closedir

```
closedir(FILEHANDLE);
```
Just like the `open` function had to be closed, now the `opendir` function must be closed.

readdir

The `readdir` function gives us a list of all the files and directories contained in the FILEHANDLE specified. When used in a scalar context, `readdir` returns the next filename. When using `readdir` in an array context, all remaining files and directories are placed into an array as a list with one name per element. Also, the order in which the files and directories are given corresponds exactly to the order in which the filesystem stores the files and directories. Here are some examples:

```
opendir(DIR, ".");
foreach $name (readdir(DIR))
{
    print "$name\n";
}
closedir(DIR);
```

This prints out every file and directory residing in the current directory (.). We can also use the `sort` command to display the names sorted alphabetically; simply replace the second line with:

```
foreach $name (sort readdir(DIR))
```

Also, we can put the contents of a directory into an array like this:

```
@files = sort readdir(DIR);
```

push

The `push` command simply adds a scalar value to the end of an array.

```
push(@thisarray, $somevalue);
```

So, if the elements of `@thisarray` were (1, 2, 3, 4), then after executing this line `@thisarray` would contain (1, 2, 3, 4, $somevalue).

pop

Although not used in this script, the `pop` command does the exact opposite of `push`: It removes the last element of an array and returns it.

```
$lastelement = pop(@thisarray);
```

subroutines

Subroutines are a series of functions that perform a particular task or set of tasks. This is a good way to set up a subroutine that you can call from within the script every time you need it rather than writing it out every time you use it.

Syntax

```
sub some_name
{
    statements;
}
```

Use `&subroutine_name;` to call the subroutine.

Now you're ready to write your first interface to enter content and have it sent to the script.

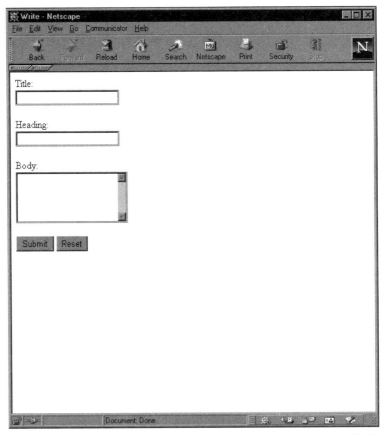

FIGURE 1–1 Interface to the write.cgi script. The contents of these fields will be parsed to write.cgi and then displayed in a list.

HTML for 1–5
write.html

```
<HTML>
<HEAD>
```

```
<TITLE>Write</TITLE>
</HEAD>

<BODY>
<FORM METHOD="POST" ACTION="write.cgi">
<P>Title:<BR>
<INPUT TYPE="text" NAME="title" SIZE"20"></P>

<P>Heading:<BR>
<INPUT TYPE="text" NAME="heading" SIZE="20"></P>

<P>Body:<BR>
<TEXTAREA ROWS="4" NAME="body" COLS="20"
WRAP="virtual"></TEXTAREA></P>

<P><INPUT TYPE="submit" VALUE="Submit" NAME="submit">
<INPUT TYPE="reset" VALUE="Reset"  NAME="reset"></P>
</FORM>
</BODY>
</HTML>
```

Script 1–5
write.cgi

```
    #!/usr/bin/perl
1.  &get_form_data;
    print "Content-type: text/html\n\n";
2.  opendir(DIR, "./numbers");
3.  while($name = readdir(DIR))
    {
4.      next if $name !~ /^\d*.html/;
5.      push(@files, $name);
    }
6.  close(DIR);
7.  if($#files == 0)
    {
8.      $nextfile = "1.html";
    }
9.  else
    {
10.     $lastfile = $files[$#files];
11.     $lastfile =~ s/.html//g;
12.     $nextfile = $lastfile + 1;
13.     $nextfile .= ".html";
    }
14. open(OUT, ">numbers/$nextfile");
15. print OUT "<HTML>\n<HEAD>\n ";
16. print OUT "<TITLE>\n";
17. print OUT "$FORM{'title'}\n";
18. print OUT "</TITLE>\n";
```

```
19.  print OUT "</HEAD>\n";
20.  print OUT "<BODY BGCOLOR=\"#FFFFFF\">\n";
21.  print OUT "<H1>\n";
22.  print OUT "$FORM{'heading'}\n";
23.  print OUT "</H1>\n";
24.  print OUT "<P>\n";
25.  print OUT "$FORM{'body'}\n";
26.  close(OUT);
27.  push(@files, $nextfile);
28.  print "<HTML>\n<BODY>\n";
29.  foreach $file (@files)
     {
30.     print "<A HREF=\"numbers/$file\">$file</A>\n";
        print "<BR>\n";
     }
     print "</BODY>\n</HTML>\n";
31.  exit;

32.  sub get_form_data
     {
        # Get the input
        read(STDIN, $buffer, $ENV{ 'CONTENT_LENGTH' } );
        # Split the name-value pairs
        @pairs = split(/&/, $buffer);
        foreach $pair (@pairs)
        {
           ($name, $value) = split(/=/, $pair);
           # Un-Webify plus signs and %-encoding
           $value =~ tr/+/ /;
           $value =~ s/%([a-fA-F0-9][a-fA-F0-9])/pack("C",
                                          hex($1))/eg;
           $value =~ s/<!--(.|\n)*-->//g;
           $FORM{ $name } = $value;
        }
     }
```

HOW THE SCRIPT WORKS

1. `&get_form_data;` calls the subroutine `get_form_data`, which is located at the end of the script, and which parses the user output.

2. The `opendir` command gets a listing of all the files in the directory specified. The `./` command tells the script to look in the local directory in the `numbers` subdirectory and to assign `DIR` as the FILEHANDLE.

3. This loops through each file and directory in the `./numbers` directory, with `$name` containing a single file/directory for that iteration.

4. The `next` command uses regular expressions to skip this iteration of the current loop structure (the `while`) only if the file does not match (`!~`) the following:

   The beginning of the file starts with a digit (`^` means beginning of the file, `\d` means any digit from 0–9), followed by any number of digits. (The `*` matches any character. Since it follows the `\d`, it only matches more digits, instead of any character). Then, it matches .html. So, any file such as 5.html, 1231.html, 1.html, and so forth, will be matched.

5. `push` adds the filename to the `@files` array. Remember that this is only done if the regular expression in line 4 fails (that is, we don't skip through this iteration of the loop).

6. This line checks to see if the `@files` array is empty (`$#arrayname` is the length of `arrayname`).

7. If the array is empty, then this is our first run through. We do not have any files such as 1.html or 5.html.

8. If line 7 were true then we start with 1.html, by assigning it to `$nextfile`.

9. `$lastfile` is assigned the last element in the `@files` array (from line 6, `$#arrayname` is the length of the array, which is also the number of elements in the array).

10. Using regular expressions, remove `.html` from the filename.

11. Add 1 to the value of `$nextfile` (since we removed the `.html` from the filename, all we have left is a number).

12. The `.=` character is used to append `.html` to `$nextfile`.

13. Create a file with the name of the value of `$nextfile` in the `/numbers` directory.

14–25. Print out HTML content to the OUT FILEHANDLE, which appends the content to the end of the file.

26. Close the OUT FILEHANDLE.

27. Add the value of `$nextfile` to the `@files` array.

28. Print the opening HTML tags that will be shown to the browser.

29. Loop through each element in the `@files` array.

30. Print out a link to each file along with the filename itself, separated by a line break.

31. Quit executing the script.

32. The `get_form_data` function reads in the form submission content and places each value into the `%FORM` associative array.

Once you have write.cgi and write.html saved, you will use write.html to fill in the three fields (title, heading, and body) with content. Then write.cgi will be accessed and write a file using the content that was just entered (see Figure 1–2).

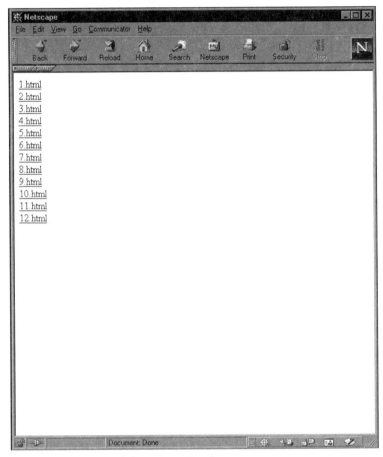

FIGURE 1–2 Results of the write.cgi script

Recap

We covered a lot in this chapter. You learned how to open and read external files and directories with the open command, as well as write new files with the write character (>), and append to a file with the append character (>>).

You have also had your first look at arrays, which you will be using more and more as we move along in the projects.

Advanced Projects

Take the random.cgi script and add at least 10 different types of messages that the script might output. Each one should be a fully coded HTML page with different type styles, colors, and graphics.

Modify the readme.cgi script so that instead of outputting a file by time of day, the script will output a different file for each of the seven days that a user will open the page. For example, if the day is Sunday, a file will write sunday.html; if it is Monday, the script will output monday.html; and so on.

2 E-mail Script!

IN THIS CHAPTER

- Project I: E-mail Script
- Quick Introduction to Forms
- E-mail Return Script
- Recap
- Advanced Projects

In the preceding chapter you learned how to open up files for reading and writing to pass information to and from the user's browser. You also learned how to use that same open *command to open directories so that you don't always have to use a file in the same directory in which your Perl script is located. Now you will go one step further into this wonderful world of using the* open *command to open programs and pass information to them. One of the most common uses for this is to open the sendmail program, so that your script can send variables to the sendmail program and e-mail the results to the address specified.*

◆ Project I: E-mail Script

Files Used		Permissions
email.html		744
email.cgi		766

The e-mail script is used on many sites and is a very effective tool for letting your readers/users send you a wide range of information about themselves or additional information they are looking for from your site. Sure, you can just set up an e-mail link on your site that will open a new e-mail message from the user's e-mail client, but having an e-mail form on your page with specific questions or information looks much more professional.

The first thing you need to decide is what kind of information you want to get from the user. You will need to get the name and e-mail address so you can correspond with the user after receiving messages. Often times you will also want to get an address and phone number, and set up a text box in which the user can speak his or her mind.

In order to set this up you will need to create two files. The first file will be the interface that users will see, which is the forms-based HTML page with all the fields for them to complete. The second file is the Perl script that will be run in the background and do all the work. Hmm . . . that kind of sounds like the relationship between you and your boss, doesn't it? OK, so maybe not everyone can relate.

◆ Quick Introduction to Forms

Although we worked with forms briefly in the preceding chapter, now we will be using most of the elements that are used in forms. With that in mind, now is a good time to go into a little more detail about all of these form properties. If you would like more information, please refer to Appendix A, "An Introduction to Forms." The HTML form e-mail.html is a good example of a feedback interface to use that captures just about all the information you will want to initially get from a user. With email.html you will have used just about all the different form field elements to show you how they are working with the script. This should make it easier for you to determine what each element is doing.

HTML for email.cgi
email.html

```
        <HTML>
        <HEAD>
        <TITLE>Stitch Email Form</TITLE>
        </HEAD>
        <BODY BGCOLOR="#FFFFFF">
        <FONT FACE="Arial">
        <P><B>Welcome to the Feedback form for Stitch Magazine
        </B></P>
  1.    <FORM ACTION="email.cgi" METHOD="POST">
        <TABLE BORDER="0" WIDTH="450" CELLSPACING="0">
         <TR>
          <TD> Name: </TD>
        <!-------------- Start of Text boxes --------------
          <TD>
  2.    <INPUT TYPE  = "text" SIZE = "40" NAME = "name"></TD>
         </TR>
         <TR>
          <TD>Company: </TD>
          <TD>
  3.    <INPUT TYPE = "text" size = "40" name = "company"></TD>
         </TR>
         <TR>
          <TD>Address: </TD>
          <TD>
  4.    <INPUT TYPE = "text" SIZE = "40" name = "address1"></TD>
         </TR>
         <TR>
          <TD>City: </TD>
          <TD>
  5.    <INPUT TYPE = "text" SIZE = "40" name = "city"></TD>
         </TR>
         <TR>
          <TD>State: </TD>
          <TD>
  6.    <INPUT TYPE = "text" SIZE = "40" name = "state"></TD>
         </TR>
        <!------------- Start of Drop down box -------------
         <TR>
          <TD>Country: </TD>
          <TD>
  7.    <SELECT NAME = "country" SIZE = "1">
  8.    <OPTION SELECTED VALUE = "">Select a country</OPTION>
  9.    <OPTION VALUE = "United States">United States</OPTION>
 10.    <OPTION VALUE = "Transylvania">Transylvania</OPTION>
 11.    <OPTION VALUE = "Switzerland">Switzerland</OPTION>
```

```
12.  <OPTION VALUE = "Tasmania ">Tasmania</OPTION>
13.  </SELECT>
      </TD>
      </TR>
     <!-------------- End of Drop down box --------------
      <TR>
      <TD>Telephone: </TD>
      <TD>
14.  <INPUT TYPE ="text" SIZE ="40" NAME = "telephone"></TD>
      </TR>
      <TR>
      <TD>Fax: </TD>
      <TD>
15.  <INPUT TYPE ="text" SIZE ="40" NAME = "fax"></TD>
      </TR>
      <TR>
      <TD>E-Mail: </TD>
      <TD>
16.  <INPUT TYPE ="text" SIZE ="40" NAME = "email"></TD>
      </TR>
      <TR>
      <TD COLSPAN = "2"> <P><B>
     <!------------- Start of Check boxes -------------->
      What services are you interested in?</B><BR>
17.  <INPUT TYPE = "checkbox" NAME = "services" VALUE =
     "Fashion updates">
      Fashion updates  

18.  <INPUT TYPE = "checkbox" NAME = "services" VALUE =
     "Newsletter">
      Newsletter</P>
     <!-------------- End of Check boxes -------------->
     <!------------ Start of Radio buttons ------------>
      <P><B>Would you like to be notified when our pages are
      updated?:</B><BR>
19.  <INPUT TYPE = "radio" NAME = "notify" VALUE = "Yes"
     checked>
      Yes  
20.  <INPUT TYPE = "radio" NAME = "notify" VALUE = "No">
     No<BR><BR>
      <B>Comments to Stitch: </B><BR>
     <!------------- End of Radio buttons -------------->
     <!-------------- Start of Comments -------------->
21.  <TEXTAREA NAME = "comments" ROWS = "6" COLS = "44"
     WRAP = "virtual">
22.  </TEXTAREA></P>
     <!--------------- End of Comments --------------->
      <P>
23.  <INPUT TYPE = "submit" NAME = "submit" VALUE = "Submit">
```

24. `<INPUT TYPE = "reset" NAME = "reset" VALUE = "Reset">`
`</TD>`
`</TR>`
`</TABLE>`
25. `</FORM>`
`</BODY>`
`</HTML>`

HOW THE HTML WORKS

1. `<FORM>` opens the form so the browser knows to expect to show form elements. `ACTION` tells the form which script it will be using. In this case you will be calling the email.cgi script. `METHOD` lets the script know that this information is using `POST`.

2–6. Text boxes: Each text box starts with the tag `<INPUT TYPE = "text"` and gets assigned a `NAME` that will be used as a reference to the script. The `VALUE` that the user types in will be put into the variable that the `NAME=` refers to when it is passed to the script.

7–13. Drop down box: The drop down box is used here to select which country the user is from. The `NAME` is set to `country`, but the `VALUE` will be either `United States`, `Transylvania`, `Switzerland`, or `Tasmania`. You surround this grouping of tags with the `SELECT` tag and assign the group a name. In this case `country` is used and will return a value of one of the countries that will be selected on line 8, so this will be the one that is initially shown. Note that its value is set to nothing. This is fine—it just means it will show the box without a value until the user clicks on it and selects one of the other values inside.

14–16. More text boxes.

17–18. Check box: The `NAME` of this set of check boxes is set to `services` and the `VALUE` will be either `Fashion updates` or `Newsletter`. The user may select one, both, or none to be passed along.

19–20. Radio button: The `NAME` has been assigned `notify` and has a `VALUE` of either `Yes` or `No`. With the `CHECKED` attribute already set in the `Yes` field, we know that this will be returned by default. The user can select either option, but must have at least one.

21–22. TEXTAREA: This is basically a big text box with several lines. Instead of using the <INPUT TYPE = "text"> tag, you will use the <TEXTAREA> tag and assign a NAME and define the height of the box with the ROWS attribute and the length with the COLS attribute. WRAP = "virtual" makes the entered content wrap at the end of the physical text area instead of scrolling horizontally forever. This can be omitted if you wish.

23. Submit button: Once this is selected, the form sends all the entered data to the script that you assigned earlier at the beginning of the form with the ACTION = tag.

24. End of Form: You always need to close the form. If you leave out this step, you risk having your form elements not appear at all in the browser.

The HTML file results are shown in Figure 2–1.

Now that you have set up a pretty interface and have included all the appropriate fields to gather the information you need from a user, you still need to do one more step: Write the script!

◆ E-mail Return Script

This is the Perl script that email.html will use to send all its information to and from the user. Besides just grabbing all the user information, it will e-mail it to an address specified within the script. This is usually the Webmaster or a person in charge of gathering this information.

NEW FEATURES

Opening Other Programs

Using the open command you can open files, directories, or even other programs. To open the sendmail program, the syntax is

```
open(FILEHANDLE, "|/usr/sbin/sendmail")
```

| is the pipe command that allows you to use another program such as sendmail. If you wish to open another program, simply substitute the path of sendmail with the path of the other program.

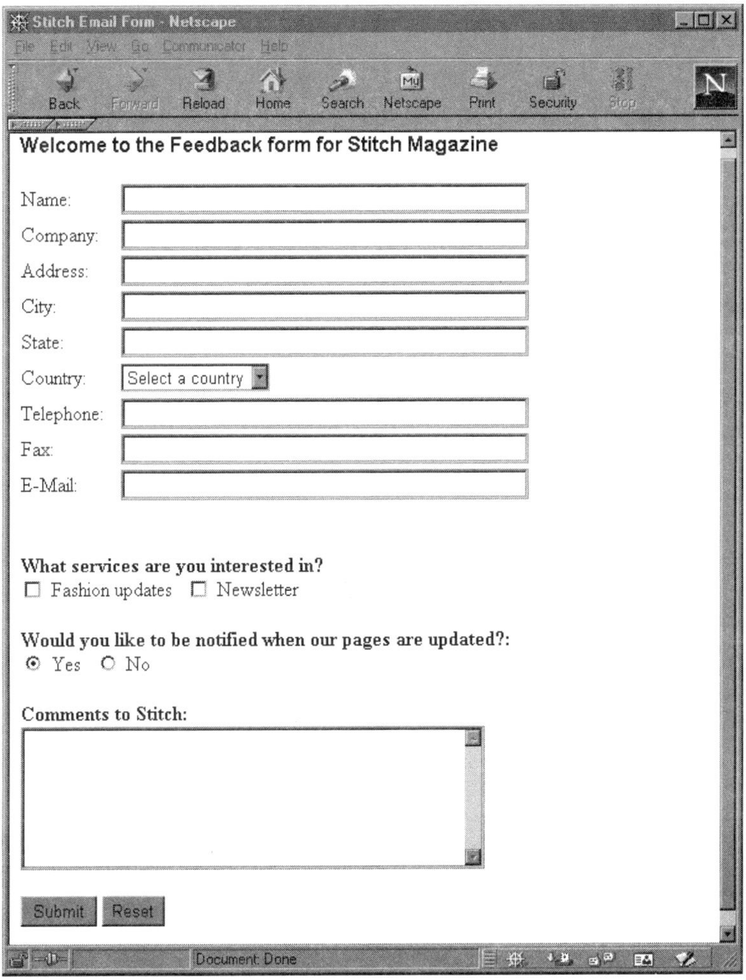

FIGURE 2–1 E-mail script results

Script 2-1
email.cgi

```perl
#!/usr/bin/perl
```
1. `&get_form_data();`
2. `&send_email;`
3. `&print_thankyou_page;`
4. `sub get_form_data`
```perl
    {
        # Get the input
```

```
        read(STDIN, $buffer, $ENV{ 'CONTENT_LENGTH' } );

        # Split the name-value pairs
        @pairs = split(/&/, $buffer);
        foreach $pair (@pairs)
        {
            ($name, $value) = split(/=/, $pair);

            # Un-Webify plus signs and %-encoding
            $value =~ tr/+/ /;
            $value =~ s/%([a-fA-F0-9][a-fA-F0-9])/pack("C",
            hex($1))/eg;
            $value =~ s/<!--(.|\n)*-->//g;
            $FORM{$name} = $value;
        }
    }
5.  sub send_email
    {
6.      $to = "user\@host.com";
7.      open(MAIL, "|/usr/sbin/sendmail -t $to") || die
        ("can't open sendmail");
8.      print MAIL "From: $FORM{'email'}\n";
9.      print MAIL "To: $to\n";
10.     print MAIL "Subject: Form submission\n\n";

        # print out the form results
11.     print MAIL "Name: $FORM{'name'}\n";
12.     print MAIL "Company: $FORM{'company'}\n";
13.     print MAIL "Address: $FORM{'address1'}\n";
14.     print MAIL "City: $FORM{'city'}\n";
15.     print MAIL "State: $FORM{'state'}\n";
16.     print MAIL "Country: $FORM{'country'}\n";
17.     print MAIL "Telephone: $FORM{'telephone'}\n";
18.     print MAIL "Fax: $FORM{'fax'}\n";
19.     print MAIL "E-mail: $FORM{'email'}\n";
20.     print MAIL "Services interested in:
        $FORM{'services'}\n";
21.     print MAIL "Notified when pages updated:
        $FORM{'notify'}\n";
22.     print MAIL "Comments: $FORM{'comments'}\n";
23.     close(MAIL);
    }

24. sub print_thankyou_page
    {
25.     print "Content-type: text/html\n\n";
26.     print "<HTML>\n<HEAD>\n<BODY BGCOLOR=\"#FFFFFF\">\n
        </HEAD>";
27.     print "<H3>Thank you</H3>\n\n";
```

```
28.     print "<P>\n";
29.     print "Thank you for your submission\n";
30.     print "<P>\n";
31.     print "<A HREF=\"some_page.html\">Return</A> to the
        home page\n";
}
32. print "</BODY<\n</HTML>";
```

HOW THE SCRIPT WORKS

1–3. This script will consist of these three subroutine calls:

```
&get_form_data();
&send_email;
&print_thankyou_page;
```

First you need to tell the script to expect the subroutines.

To call a subroutine, simply place an ampersand (&) in front of the subroutine name:

```
&subRoutineName();
```

Now we will explain what is happening in each subroutine as it is executed.

4. sub get_form_data: The first subroutine, &get_form _data();, executes a subroutine that assembles the contents of the form submission into a hash or associative array (see Appendix B, "Stepping through the Perly Gates"). The name of this associative array is %FORM. An associative array uses a string as the subscript instead of an integer, as in a regular array.

```
$FORM{'name'} = "John Doe";
$FORM{'company'} = "ABC Productions";

print "Name is $FORM{'name'}\n";
print "Company is $FORM{'company'}\n";
```

The &get_form_data subroutine first reads in the contents of the form submission and stores it into $buffer. These contents are arranged in name-value pairs; such as:

```
name=John+Doe&position=Programmer&Company=ABC
```

It then uses the split function to split up the contents and store them as individual elements inside the @pairs array. Next, we traverse each pair, and split up the name and value with the `split` function. We then use regular expressions to un-Webify + signs (which stand for spaces) and %-encoding. Finally, we store the value in the associative array %FORM, using the name of the pair as the key (the subscript).

Now we can refer to the information entered in the form by accessing elements of the %FORM array. We refer to this information by specifying the key, or subscript, of the array. If we had a text field named FULL_NAME in our HTML page, we would access what the user entered in this field by specifying:

```
$FORM{'FULL_NAME'}
```

and so on.

5. `sub send_email`: The second subroutine, `&send_email;`, contains the code that actually sends off the e-mail.

6. First, we set the `$to` variable to the address that we want the script sent to. Notice the backslash (\) in front of the @? This is because @ is a special character that Perl uses. If you would like to use it as a standard character, such as in this case where you need it within the e-mail address, you simply put a backslash in front of it so Perl knows to interpret it as just an ordinary @. There are several cases of this that we use throughout this script as well as in just about every script throughout this book. There is a table in Appendix B that provides a complete listing of which characters need the backslash in order to print as normal ASCII characters.

7. `open(MAIL, "|/usr/sbin/sendmail -t $to") || die ("can't open sendmail");` This opens a pipe (|) to the sendmail program and will send all the following information using the MAIL FILEHANDLE. The `$to` is defined on line 6 as to what e-mail address will receive this document. The | | is the `or` command and will print the following message if the sendmail application couldn't be accessed.

8–10. Now all the necessary information is sent to sendmail, starting with From, To, and so forth. Notice how we use the `print` statement. By default, the `print` statement prints out to the standard output. The standard output is just another FILEHANDLE, like our MAIL FILEHANDLE:

```
print STDOUT "Hello world";
```

is the same as

```
print "Hello world";
```

11–22. `print MAIL "Name: $FORM{'name'}\n;` Prints the data entered into the `Name` field back in the email.html and assigns it to this `name` variable. The `NAME:` is just regular text that will be printed to give you an idea of what the question was the user was responding to.

23. Now you must close the `MAIL` FILEHANDLE, which closes the sendmail program and sends the mail.

24. `print_thankyou_page:` The last subroutine, `&print _thankyou_page;,` does just that. It prints out an HTML page that users will see when they are done. Later in the book you will learn how to print out the contents of an external HTML file, rather than including the HTML in the script itself.

Checking for Required Fields

Now that you have the e-mail script working and you are receiving information from the people visiting your Web site, you might start to discover one important thing: People are only partially filling out these forms and sending them, leaving many of the fields blank. So you, not wanting to let these people get away with this, decide you want to *require* them to fill out some of the pertinent fields before they can successfully send the e-mail form to you.

We will now modify the email.cgi script we just finished so that it ensures that all the required fields are completed before allowing the user to submit the e-mail script. It is up to you to determine which fields you want to be required fields.

To do this, we will add one more subroutine to the three we already created. This new subroutine will check to make sure the fields we specify as required have some data in them.

```
&get_form_data();
&check_required_fields;
&send_email;
&print_thankyou_page;
```

You will place the new subroutine call between the get_form_data and send_email subroutines. This will allow the user to enter the form data, and then the program will check for the required data before sending the information.

An example of the check_required_fields subroutine is shown in Figure 2–2. In this case, we have decided that the Name, Address, City, State, Country, Telephone, and E-mail Address fields are required from the user. The order of the required fields does not matter as long as they do not appear in the middle of another subroutine.

Script 2–1–1
check_required_fields.txt

```
sub check_required_fields
{
    if($FORM{'name'} eq "")
    {
        $blank_name = 1;
    }
    if($FORM{'address1'} eq "")
    {
        $blank_address1 = 1;
    }
    if($FORM{'city'} eq "")
    {
        $blank_city = 1;
    }
    if($FORM{'state'} eq "")
    {
        $blank_state = 1;
    }
    if($FORM{'country'} eq "")
    {
        $blank_country = 1;
    }
    if($FORM{'telephone'} eq "")
    {
        $blank_telephone = 1;
    }
    if($FORM{'email'} eq "")
    {
        $blank_email = 1;
    }
```

```
if($blank_name || $blank_address1 || $blank_city ||
    $blank_state || $blank_country || $blank_telephone
    || $blank_email)
{
    &print_error_page;
    exit;
}
} # end sub check_required_fields
```

Notice that four lines from the bottom we make a call to a new subroutine, &print_error_page, that was not in the list of subroutines in the beginning of the script. We can simply call the &print_error_page subroutine if any of the required variables evaluate as true (see Figure 2–2).

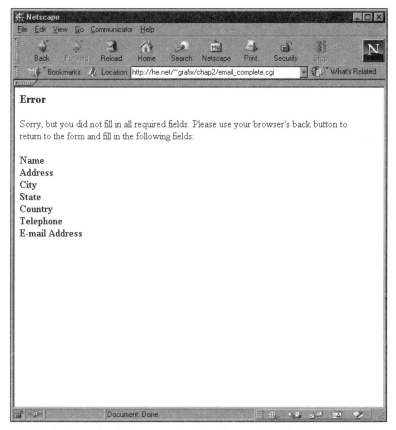

FIGURE 2–2 Result of the error checking if a required field is not filled in

Script 2–1–2
error_page.txt

```
sub print_error_page
{
   print "Content-type: text/html\n\n";
   print "<HTML>\n<BODY BGCOLOR=\"#FFFFFF\">\n\n";
   print "<H3>\n";
   print "Error\n";
   print "</H3>\n";
   print "<P>\n";
   print "Sorry, but you did not fill in all required
   fields. Please use your browser's back button\n";
   print "to return to the form and fill in the
   following fields:\n\n";
   print "<P>\n";

   print "<B>\n";
   if($blank_name)
   {
      print "Name\n";
      print "<BR>\n";
   }
   if($blank_address1)
   {
      print "Address\n";
      print "<BR>\n";
   }
   if($blank_city)
   {
      print "City\n";
      print "<BR>\n";
   }
   if($blank_state)
   {
      print "State\n";
      print "<BR>\n";
   }
   if($blank_country)
   {
      print "Country\n";
      print "<BR>\n";
   }
   if($blank_telephone)
   {
      print "Telephone\n";
      print "<BR>\n";
   }
```

```
if($blank_email)
{
    print "E-mail Address\n";
    print "<BR>\n";
}

# close out the page

print "\n\n";
print "</BODY>\n";
print "</HTML>\n";
} # end sub print_error_page
```

HOW THE SCRIPT WORKS

In the check_required_fields subroutine, we are first checking to see if any of the required fields are empty.

For example, we will look at name:

```
if($FORM{'name'} eq "")
{
    $blank_name = 1;
}
```

This if statement checks to see if the value of name is equal to nothing (" "). If this is true, then it sets the value of $blank_name to 1, for later testing. If name does have something entered then the if statement is bypassed and goes to the next if to be checked.

The next part of the test comes to these lines:

```
if($blank_name || $blank_address1 || $blank_city ||
    $blank_state || $blank_country || $blank_telephone ||
    $blank_email)
{
    &print_error_page;
    exit;
}
```

This is where the program checks to see if any of the earlier if statements were evaluated as being true. The first line of the if statement simply tests to see if any of the variables we just set are equal to 1. Here's another way to look at it:

```
if(1 || 0 || 0 || 1 || 1 || 0)
```

If any of the values are set to 1 (true), the program goes to the &print_error_page, then exits.

If all fields were filled in and evaluated as false, the program will keep moving right along.

sub print_error_page

The print_error_page subroutine will print out the header HTML, and then check to see which of those variables we set in the check_required_fields subroutine are set to 1. The program will print out the name of each variable that is set to 1, thereby notifying the user of the missing information for the required field(s).

Passing Variables Back to the User

Sub print_return_page

The print_return_page subroutine returns an HTML page that contains the information the user submitted, and has been e-mailed to the address you have specified. Note that the lines that actually print out the form contents look almost exactly like the lines that do the same thing in the e-mail subroutine, only those print to the MAIL FILEHANDLE instead of the default FILEHANDLE STDOUT (standard output, or your screen). The exact syntax for the print statement is

```
print FILEHANDLE output;
```

By not specifying the FILEHANDLE, the default FILEHANDLE STDOUT is used, sending output to the user's screen.

Since you are using the subroutine print_return_page, you can get rid of the print_thankyou_page subroutine that was used earlier (see Figure 2–3).

Script 2–1–3
return_page.txt

```
sub print_return_page
{
    print "<HTML>\n<BODY BGCOLOR=\"#FFFFFF\">\n";
    print "<H3>\n";
    print "Thank you\n";
    print "</H3>\n\n";
    print "The following information has been e-mailed
    to: ";
    print $to;
```

```
        print "\n<P>\n";
        print "Name: $FORM{'name'}<BR>";
        print "Company: $FORM{'company'}<BR> ";
        print "Address: $FORM{'address1'}<BR>";
        print "City: $FORM{'city'}<BR>";
        print "State: $FORM{'state'}<BR>";
        print "Country: $FORM{'country'}<BR>";
        print "Telephone: $FORM{'telephone'}<BR>";
        print "Fax: $FORM{'fax'}<BR>";
        print "E-mail: $FORM{'email'}<BR>";
        print "Services interested in:
$FORM{'services'}<BR>";
        print "Notified when pages updated:
$FORM{'notify'}<BR>";
        print "Comments: $FORM{'comments'}<BR>";
        print "<P><BR>";
        print "</BODY>\n</HTML><BR>";
        exit;
}
```

FIGURE 2–3 Results passed back to the user

Writing the Results to a File (Comma and Tab Delimited)

The subroutine `sub log_data` saves the contents of the information submitted to a comma-delimited file. This means that each line in this new comma-delimited file will contain the contents of a single submission, with each field separated by a comma. This data can then be imported into many different types of databases for various analyzation tasks.

Since you will be opening this new file constantly to write to, you might want to consider what would happen if two people were to write to the file through the e-mail script at the same moment. While the chances of this occurring are remote, the fact is that it might, so you will want to take precautions to make certain this doesn't happen. This is done with the `flock` function.

NEW FUNCTIONS

flock

`flock` is used to lock a file so that nothing else can write to it except the script that locked it.

```
flock(FILEHANDLE, "FILE_LOCKING_NAME");
```

Name	Operation	Function
Lock_sh	1	Creates a shared lock
Lock_ex	2	Creates an exclusive lock
Lock_nb	4	Creates a nonblocking lock
Lock_un	8	Unlocks an existing lock

Example

```
$lock_ex = 2;
$lock_un = 8;
open(FILEHANDLE, ">>file.txt");
flock(FILEHANDLE, "$lock_ex");
#locks the file so others can't write to it
print "FILEHANDLE, "something";
flock "(FILEHANDLE, "$lock_un"); #unlocks the file
```

To add this functionality you need to add this new subroutine to the end of the email.cgi script and also add the `&log_data` in the beginning of the script under the other subroutine calls to let the script call this new subroutine. It should look like this:

```
&get_form_data();
&check_required_fields;
&send_email;
&print_thankyou_page;
&log_data;
```

Script 2-1-4
log_data.txt

```
1.   sub log_data
     {
2.     $lock_ex = 2;
3.     $lock_un = 8;
4.     open(OUT, ">>logfile.txt");
5.     flock(OUT, "$lock_ex");
6.     print OUT $FORM{'name'};
7.     print OUT ",";
       print OUT $FORM{'company'};
       print OUT ",";
       print OUT $FORM{'address1'};
       print OUT ",";
       print OUT $FORM{'city'};
       print OUT ",";
       print OUT $FORM{'state'};
       print OUT ",";
       print OUT $FORM{'country'};
       print OUT ",";
       print OUT $FORM{'telephone'};
       print OUT ",";
       print OUT $FORM{'fax'};
       print OUT ",";
       print OUT $FORM{'email'};
       print OUT ",";
       print OUT $FORM{'services'};
       print OUT ",";
       print OUT $FORM{'notify'};
       print OUT ",";
       print OUT $FORM{'comments'};
8.     print OUT "\n";
9.     close(OUT);
10.    flock(OUT, "$lock_un");
     }
```

HOW THE SCRIPT WORKS

1. Specifies the name of this subroutine as log_data.

2. Set $lock_ex to the value of 2, "exclusive lock."

3. Set $lock_un to the value of 8, "unlock the existing lock."

4. Opens the file logfile.txt to have the contents of your email.cgi script appended to it and uses OUT as the FILE-HANDLE.

5. Call the flock function and assign the FILEHANDLE as well as the type of flock to use. In this case, you are calling $lock_ex, which has the value of 2, exclusive lock.

6. Print the form field name to the OUT FILEHANDLE. The text between the single quotes corresponds to the NAME="" HTML tag in the preceding form.

7. Print out the rest of the form contents, separating each field with a comma. If you're worried about people entering commas in the fields, then this could pose a problem since this will throw off the fields. To correct this you could very easily turn this into a tab-delimited file by using the \t special character in place of the commas. Simply change the line from

```
print OUT ",";
```

to

```
print OUT "\t";
```

8. This is the end of this record, so print a newline so the file is ready for another record.

9. Close the FILEHANDLE.

10. Call the flock once again, only this time you are calling $lock_un, which has the value of 8, unlock the existing lock.

Modified E-mail Script

Now that you have gone through adding the error checking to make sure that certain fields of information were filled out, returned the filled out information to the user and logged the data, you have a pretty happening script going on here. Since you will be checking to see if the required fields are actually being filled out before you print a thank-you page and log the comments, the order must change slightly or things will not work out as you had planned. First, you will need to check to see if any required fields have not been filled out before the other routines such as send_email, print_return_page, and log_data. To do this you will move the `check_required_fields` subroutine to execute right after the `get_form_data` is finished parsing the user's data. If all the conditions are met, the script moves to the next routines with the `else` command. Here is what the code looks like when it is completely written out:

Script 2-2
email_complete.cgi

```perl
#!/usr/bin/perl
&get_form_data();
&check_required_fields;

sub check_required_fields
{
    if($FORM{'name'} eq "")
    {
        $blank_name = 1;
    }
    if($FORM{'address1'} eq "")
    {
        $blank_address1 = 1;
    }
    if($FORM{'city'} eq "")
    {
        $blank_city = 1;
    }
    if($FORM{'state'} eq "")
    {
        $blank_state = 1;
    }
    if($FORM{'country'} eq "")
    {
        $blank_country = 1;
    }
    if($FORM{'telephone'} eq "")
    {
        $blank_telephone = 1;
    }
    if($FORM{'email'} eq "")
    {
        $blank_email = 1;
    }
} # end sub check_required_fields

if($blank_name || $blank_address1 || $blank_city ||
    $blank_state || $blank_country || $blank_telephone ||
    $blank_email)
```

```perl
{
    &print_error_page;
    exit;
}
else
{
    &send_email;
    &print_return_page;
    &log_data;
    exit;
}

sub get_form_data
{
    # Get the input
    read(STDIN, $buffer, $ENV{ 'CONTENT_LENGTH' } );

    # Split the name-value pairs
    @pairs = split(/&/, $buffer);
    foreach $pair (@pairs)
    {
        ($name, $value) = split(/=/, $pair);

        # Un-Webify plus signs and %-encoding
        $value =~ tr/+/ /;
        $value =~ s/%([a-fA-F0-9][a-fA-F0-9])/pack("C",
        hex($1))/eg;
        $value =~ s/<!--(.|\n)*-->//g;
        $FORM{$name} = $value;
    }
}
sub send_email
{
    $to = "user\@host.com";
    open(MAIL, "|/usr/sbin/sendmail -t $to") || die
    ("can't open sendmail");
    print MAIL "From: $FORM{'email'}\n";
    print MAIL "To: $to\n";
    print MAIL "Subject: Form submission\n\n";

    # print out the form results
    print MAIL "Name: $FORM{'name'}\n";
    print MAIL "Company: $FORM{'company'}\n";
    print MAIL "Address: $FORM{'address1'}\n";
    print MAIL "City: $FORM{'city'}\n";
    print MAIL "State: $FORM{'state'}\n";
    print MAIL "Country: $FORM{'country'}\n";
    print MAIL "Telephone: $FORM{'telephone'}\n";
    print MAIL "Fax: $FORM{'fax'}\n";
```

```perl
    print MAIL "E-mail: $FORM{'email'}\n";
    print MAIL "Services interested in:
    $FORM{'services'}\n";
    print MAIL "Notified when pages updated:
    $FORM{'notify'}\n";
    print MAIL "Comments: $FORM{'comments'}\n";
    close(MAIL);
}

sub print_error_page
{
    print "Content-type: text/html\n\n";
    print "<HTML>\n<BODY BGCOLOR=\"#FFFFFF\">\n\n";
    print "<H3>\n";
    print "Error\n";
    print "</H3>\n";
    print "<P>\n";
    print "Sorry, but you did not fill in all required
    fields. Please use your browser's back button\n";
    print "to return to the form and fill in the
    following fields:\n\n";
    print "<P>\n";

    print "<B>\n";
    if($blank_name)
    {
        print "Name\n";
        print "<BR>\n";
    }
    if($blank_address1)
    {
        print "Address\n";
        print "<BR>\n";
    }
    if($blank_city)
    {
        print "City\n";
        print "<BR>\n";
    }
    if($blank_state)
    {
        print "State\n";
        print "<BR>\n";
    }
    if($blank_country)
    {
        print "Country\n";
        print "<BR>\n";
    }
```

```perl
      if($blank_telephone)
      {
         print "Telephone\n";
         print "<BR>\n";
      }
      if($blank_email)
      {
         print "E-mail Address\n";
         print "<BR>\n";
      }

      # close out the page

      print "\n\n";
      print "</BODY>\n";
      print "</HTML>\n";

} # end sub print_error_page

sub print_return_page
{
      print "Content-type: text/html\n\n";
      print "<HTML>\n<BODY BGCOLOR=\"#FFFFFF\">\n";
      print "<H3>\n";
      print "Thank you\n";
      print "</H3>\n\n";
      print "The following information has been e-mailed
      to: ";
      print $to;
      print "\n<P>\n";
      print "Name: $FORM{'name'}<BR>";
      print "Company: $FORM{'company'}<BR>";
      print "Address: $FORM{'address1'}<BR>";
      print "City: $FORM{'city'}<BR>";
      print "State: $FORM{'state'}<BR>";
      print "Country: $FORM{'country'}<BR>";
      print "Telephone: $FORM{'telephone'}<BR>";
      print "Fax: $FORM{'fax'}<BR>";
      print "E-mail: $FORM{'email'}<BR>";
      print "Services interested in:
      $FORM{'services'}<BR>";
```

```
    print "Notified when pages updated:
$FORM{'notify'}<BR>";
    print "Comments: $FORM{'comments'}<BR>";
    print "<P><BR>";
    print "</BODY>\n</HTML><BR>";
}

sub log_data
{
    $lock_ex = 2;
    $lock_un = 8;
    open(OUT, ">>logfile.txt");
    flock(OUT, "$lock_ex");
    print OUT $FORM{'name'};
    print OUT ",";
    print OUT $FORM{'company'};
    print OUT ",";
    print OUT $FORM{'address1'};
    print OUT ",";
    print OUT $FORM{'city'};
    print OUT ",";
    print OUT $FORM{'state'};
    print OUT ",";
    print OUT $FORM{'country'};
    print OUT ",";
    print OUT $FORM{'telephone'};
    print OUT ",";
    print OUT $FORM{'fax'};
    print OUT ",";
    print OUT $FORM{'email'};
    print OUT ",";
    print OUT $FORM{'services'};
    print OUT ",";
    print OUT $FORM{'notify'};
    print OUT ",";
    print OUT $FORM{'comments'};
    print OUT "\n";
    close(OUT);
    flock(OUT, "$lock_un");
}
```

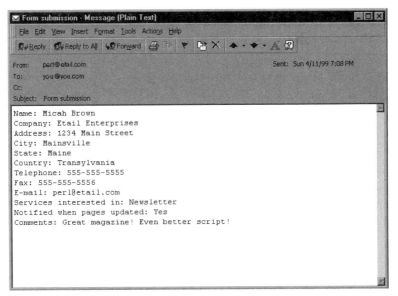

FIGURE 2-4 This is what your e-mail will look like when a user submits the e-mail

RECAP

In this chapter you have learned how to successfully set up an e-mail response form to gather information from people who are visiting your site. You learned a little about how subroutines can do different functions and interact with each other.

More importantly you have learned how to check fields to ensure that data is being entered before it is passed through to the sendmail program.

And finally, you have seen how once this form has been completed and sent, the variables are passed back to the screen.

ADVANCED PROJECTS

Add a few more fields to the email.cgi script to include items such as radio buttons to have users specify if they are male or female, and have them enter their favorite color. Also have the last subroutine you learned about, log_data, separate the fields by writing each field to a newline and the last line to add a double newline character.

3 Interacting with Users

IN THIS CHAPTER

- Project I: Write a Guestbook
- Project II: Multiple Choice Logging Poll or Voting Booth
- Project III: Quiz
- Recap
- Advanced Projects

Now that you've won the hearts and minds of upper management, who think you're a cybergod for setting up an interactive way for Web site users to send personalized information to you that can be added to your readership database, they want more. You're up for the challenge, right?

In this chapter we will be covering three interactive scripts that allow input from your users that will decide the output. The first is a guestbook script that will allow users to insert information into four fields: Name, E-mail, Company, and Comments. With the guestbook script you will be using two separate HTML files: first, the guestbook.html file for the user to input the information, and second, guestbook-view.html, which will be used to display previous entries.

◆ Project I: Write a Guestbook

Files Used	Permissions
guestbook.html	644
guestbook-view.html	766
get_form_data.pl	755
guestbook-save.cgi	755

HTML 3–1
guestbook.html

```
<HTML>
<HEAD>
<TITLE>
Guestbook
</TITLE>
</HEAD>
<BODY BGCOLOR="#FFFFFF">
<H2>A Simple Guestbook</H2>
<FORM ACTION="guestbook-save.cgi" METHOD="POST">
Name:
<INPUT TYPE="TEXT" NAME="NAME">
<P>
E-mail Address:
<BR>
<INPUT TYPE="TEXT" NAME="EMAIL">
<P>
Company:
<BR>
<INPUT TYPE="TEXT" NAME="COMPANY">
<P>
Comments:
<BR>
<TEXTAREA NAME="COMMENTS" ROWS="4" COLS="50"
WRAP="virtual">
</TEXTAREA>
<P>
<INPUT TYPE="SUBMIT" VALUE="Submit">
<INPUT TYPE="RESET" VALUE="Clear">
</FORM>
</BODY>
</HTML>
```

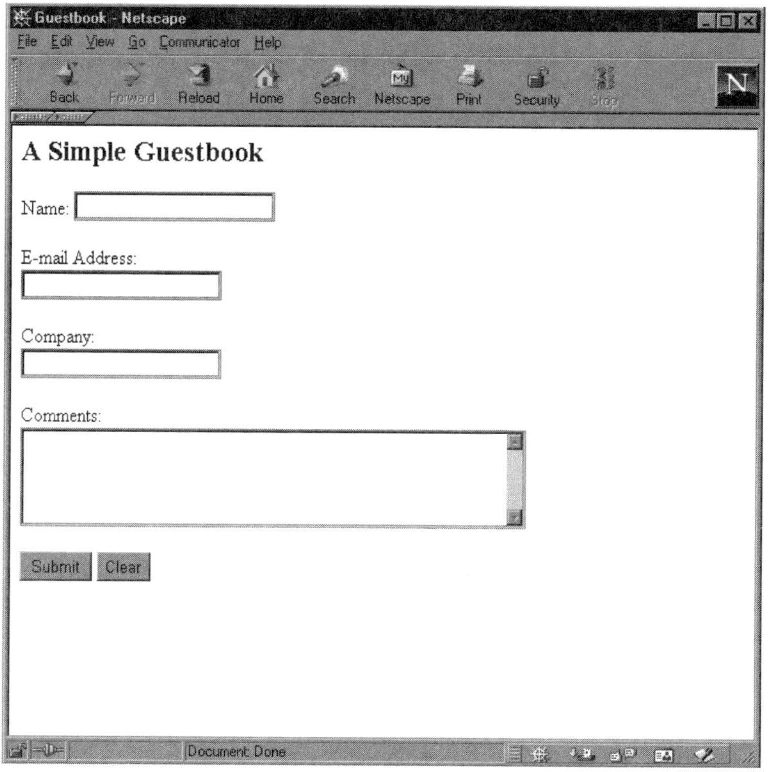

FIGURE 3-1 Interface of the guestbook script

This file is just a normal HTML file, which submits form data to guestbook-save.cgi. In this case, it will be submitting the contents of the Name, E-mail, Company, and Comments fields. The guestbook-save.cgi script does just that, it takes the form data from guestbook.html, and processes and saves it to guestbook-view.html.

HTML 3-2
guestbook-view.html

```
<HTML>
<HEAD>
<TITLE>
My Guestbook
</TITLE>
</HEAD>
<BODY BGCOLOR="#FFFFFF">
<H2>What others have to say...</H2>
```

```
<!-- start here -->
<P>
<A HREF="guestbook.html">Back to the guestbook</A>
</BODY>
</HTML>
```

Note that the line `<!-- start here -->` is just an HTML comment tag that will not be displayed to your browser. It simply gives you a place to mark where you want to place the guestbook entries.

Now take a look at the heart of all this, the guestbook-save.cgi script.

NEW FEATURES

require

The `require` function is used to call another Perl script to use routines that are included within that file. This is a great way to modularize your scripts. For the course of the book, the form

FIGURE 3–2 After one entry has been submitted to the guestbook script

parsing routine will be placed on its own in a file called `get_form_data.pl` so it can be called at the beginning of each script without actually existing within that script, thus saving you from rewriting it into each script. Another benefit of this is that if you were to make a change to `get_form_data.pl`, the change would be updated throughout each script, whereas if you were to have this routine in each script, you would have to change it for each one.

Additionally, you can hold several subroutines within a separate file and call the routine you need. You could even have several subroutines within this document that one file calls but another does not. If it isn't called, it simply isn't used.

Syntax

```
require "get_form_data.pl";
```

Script 3–1
get_form_data.pl

```
sub get_form_data
{
    # Get the input
    read(STDIN, $buffer, $ENV{ 'CONTENT_LENGTH' } );

    # Split the name-value pairs
    @pairs = split(/&/, $buffer);
    foreach $pair (@pairs)
    {
        ($name, $value) = split(/=/, $pair);

        # Un-Webify plus signs and %-encoding
        $value =~ tr/+/ /;
        $value =~ s/%([a-fA-F0-9][a-fA-F0-9])/pack("C",
        hex($1))/eg;
        $value =~ s/<!--(.|\n)*-->//g;

        if($FORM{$name} ne "")
        {
            $FORM{$name} .= "; $value";
        } else
        {
            $FORM{$name} = $value;
        }
    }
}
1;
```

The `get_form_data.pl` only holds the form parsing routine that you will be using for the rest of the book. You will now only need to write it out one time; in your future scripts you can simply call it by using the `require` function followed by `&get_form_data;`, which calls the name of this routine in that file.

Script 3–2
guestbook-save.cgi

```perl
1.  #!/usr/bin/perl
2.  require "get_form_data.pl";
3.  &get_form_data;
4.  print "Content-type: text/html\n\n";
5.  open(GUESTBOOK_IN, "./guestbook-view.html");
6.  while(<GUESTBOOK_IN>)
7.  {
8.     push(@guestbook, $_);
9.  }
10. close(GUESTBOOK_IN);
11. open(GUESTBOOK_OUT, ">./guestbook-view.html");
12. $entry = "";
13. foreach $line (@guestbook)
14. {
15.    if($line ne "<!-- start here -->\n")
16.    {
17.       print GUESTBOOK_OUT $line;
18.    } else
19.    {
20.       print GUESTBOOK_OUT $line;
21.       $entry .= "\n\n";
22.       $entry .= "Name: $FORM{'NAME'} <<A 23.HREF=\
              "mailto:$FORM{'EMAIL'}\">$FORM{'EMAIL'}</A>>\n";
23.       $entry .= "<BR>\n";
24.       $entry .= "Company: $FORM{'COMPANY'}\n";
25.       $entry .= "<BR>\n";
26.       $entry .= "Comments:\n";
27.       $entry .= "<BR>\n";
28.       $FORM{'COMMENTS'} =~ s/\s/\n<BR>/;
29.       $entry .= $FORM{'COMMENTS'};
30.       $entry .= "\n\n<HR>\n";
31.       print GUESTBOOK_OUT $entry;
32.    }
33. }
34. close(GUESTBOOK_OUT);
35. open(GUESTBOOK, "./guestbook-view.html");
36. while(<GUESTBOOK>)
37. {
38.    print $_;
```

39. }
40. close (GUESTBOOK);
41. exit;

HOW THE SCRIPT WORKS

2. require "get_form_data.pl"; Tells the script that it will be using some of the get_form_data.pl script.

3. &get_form_data; Tells the script that it will be using the get_form_data subroutine from the get_form_data.pl script.

4. Print the Content-type to let the browser know what type of data to expect.

5. Opens the guestbook-view.html file and assigns it the FILEHANDLE GUESTBOOK_IN.

6. While the GUESTBOOK_IN FILEHANDLE is open, the contents are placed into the @guestbook array.

7. Close the GUESTBOOK_IN FILEHANDLE.

8. Opens the GUESTBOOK_OUT FILEHANDLE, which you'll use to write the data out to the guestbook-view.html file with the push command.

10. Close the GUESTBOOK_IN FILEHANDLE.

11. Opens a new FILEHANDLE called GUESTBOOK_OUT and writes to the guestbook-view.html file.

12. $entry variable gets initialized here. This variable will be used to construct the entries to the guestbook-view.html file in lines 21–30.

13–33. foreach $line (@guestbook) loops through each line in the @guestbook array. Each time a new line from the guestbook file is looked at, it is tested to see if it is at the line with the comment <!--start here--> mentioned on line 15. If it's not at that line, it simply prints out the current line to the new guestbook file (remember that since it opened the GUESTBOOK_OUT FILEHANDLE for write, it overwrote the original file. That is why you put the contents of guestbook-view.html into the @guestbook array.)

20–31. This block is only executed when we find that our current position in the @guestbook array is the line with the comment on it.

20. First, we print out the comment line to the guestbook HTML file, because we want to place the most recent entry on top.

21–30. This constructs the $entry variable, which contains all the form elements in the format we want it to be in. Notice line 28. The COMMENTS field is a text box. Line 28 uses regular expressions to replace a carriage return (\s) with a newline (\n) + a <BR>, so the field is displayed correctly in the browser. Otherwise, with just a carriage return, the COMMENTS field will appear on just one line, because HTML doesn't display carriage returns or newlines. We will discuss regular expression in Chapter 4, "Searching the Web."

31. Here we print out this constructed entry to the guestbook HTML file.

34. We close out the HTML file.

35–39. Finally, we open the HTML file we just edited and print out the contents to the browser. This way, the HTML file we edited becomes our return page.

40. Close the GUESTBOOK FILEHANDLE.

41. Exit the script.

◆ Project II: Multiple Choice Logging Poll or Voting Booth

Files Used	Permissions
poll.html	644
poll.cgi	755
poll.dat	644
get_form_data.cgi	755

With the preceding script we were able to add comments to a file to then be displayed to an HTML file. What if you wanted to take a series of Yes and No or 1, 2, and 3 type answers and append them to poll the results of an online questionnaire?

Start with poll.html, which will contain a form with three questions. This HTML file will submit the results to the poll.cgi script, which will save the answers to the questions in poll.dat, a text file you will construct from within poll.cgi to store all answers. The answers will be saved by taking the existing value in that text file and adding a 1 to it. For instance, the value of the first question is "What is your favorite color?" There are three possible answers: Blue, Red, and Other. All of these values are initially set to 0, but if a user selects Red as a favorite color, then the value becomes 1.

Choice	Initial Value	New Value
Blue	0	0
Red	0	1
Other	0	0

HTML 3–3
poll.html

```
<HTML>
<HEAD>
<TITLE>
Multiple Choice Logging Poll
</TITLE>
</HEAD>
<BODY BGCOLOR="#FFFFFF">
<FORM ACTION="poll.cgi" METHOD="POST">
<H2>Multiple Choice Logging Poll</H2>
<P>
What is your favorite color?:
<BR>
<INPUT TYPE="RADIO" NAME="COLOR" VALUE="Blue">Blue
<BR>
<INPUT TYPE="RADIO" NAME="COLOR" VALUE="Red">Red
<BR>
<INPUT TYPE="RADIO" NAME="COLOR" VALUE="Other">Other
<P>
What is your favorite fruit?:
<BR>
<INPUT TYPE="RADIO" NAME="FRUIT" VALUE="Apple">Apple
<BR>
<INPUT TYPE="RADIO" NAME="FRUIT" VALUE="Orange">Orange
<P>
```

```
I use the Internet:
<BR>
<INPUT TYPE="RADIO" NAME="INTERNET" VALUE="0-5">0-5
hours per week
<BR>
<INPUT TYPE="RADIO" NAME="INTERNET" VALUE="6-10">6-10
hours per week
<BR>
<INPUT TYPE="RADIO" NAME="INTERNET" VALUE="11+">11+
hours per week
<P>
<INPUT TYPE="SUBMIT" VALUE="Submit">
</FORM>
</BODY>
</HTML>
```

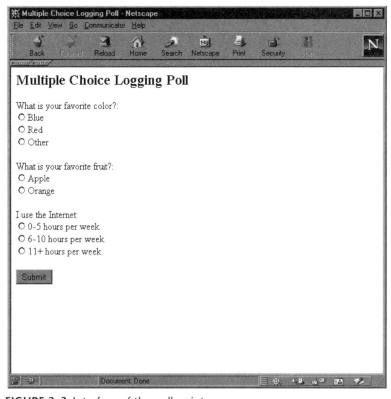

FIGURE 3–3 Interface of the poll script

Script 3–3
poll.cgi

```perl
1.  #!/usr/bin/perl
2.  require "get_form_data.pl";
3.  &get_form_data;
4.  print "Content-type: text/html\n\n";
5.  if(-e "poll.dat")
6.  {
7.     open(POLL, "poll.dat");
8.  }

9.  while(<POLL>)
10. {
11.    push(@poll, $_);
12. }
13. close(POLL);

14. @lines = ("1", "2", "3");
15. foreach $each_line (@lines)
16. {
17.    $this_line = "line" . $each_line;
18.    $$this_line = $poll[$each_line-1];
19.    chop($$this_line);
20. }
21. if($line1 eq "")
22. {
23.    $line1 = "0\t0\t0";
24. }
25. if($line2 eq "")
26. {
27.    $line2 = "0\t0";
28. }
29. if($line3 eq "")
30. {
31.    $line3 = "0\t0\t0";
32. }
33. @line1_answers = split(/\t/, $line1);
34. @line2_answers = split(/\t/, $line2);
35. @line3_answers = split(/\t/, $line3);
36. if($FORM{'COLOR'} eq "Blue")
37. {
38.    $line1_answers[0]++;
39. }
40. elsif($FORM{'COLOR'} eq "Red")
41. {
42.    $line1_answers[1]++;
43. }
```

```
44.  elsif($FORM{'COLOR'} eq "Other")
45.  {
46.     $line1_answers[2]++;
47.  }
48.  if($FORM{'FRUIT'} eq "Apple")
49.  {
50.     $line2_answers[0]++;
51.  }
52.  elsif($FORM{'FRUIT'} eq "Orange")
53.  {
54.     $line2_answers[1]++;
55.  }
56.  if($FORM{'INTERNET'} eq "0-5")
57.  {
58.     $line3_answers[0]++;
59.  }
60.  elsif($FORM{'INTERNET'} eq "6-10")
61.  {
62.     $line3_answers[1]++;
63.  }
64.  elsif($FORM{'INTERNET'} eq "11+")
65.  {
66.     $line3_answers[2]++;
67.  }

68.  open(POLL, ">poll.dat");
69.  print POLL
     "$line1_answers[0]\t$line1_answers[1]\t$line1_answers[2]\n";
70.  print POLL "$line2_answers[0]\t$line2_answers[1]\n";
71.  print POLL
     "$line3_answers[0]\t$line3_answers[1]\t$line3_answers[2]\n";
72.  close(POLL);

73.  print <<EOF;
74.  <HTML>
75.  <HEAD>
76.  <TITLE>
77.  Multiple Choice Logging Poll
78.  </TITLE>
79.  </HEAD>
80.  <BODY BGCOLOR="#FFFFFF">
81.  <H2>Multiple Choice Logging Poll</H2>
82.  <P>
83.  EOF
84.  print "What is your favorite color?:\n<BR>\n";
85.  print "Blue: ";
86.  print $line1_answers[0];
87.  print "\n<BR>\n";
88.  print "Red: ";
```

```
 89.  print $line1_answers[1];
 90.  print "\n<BR>\n";
 91.  print "Other: ";
 92.  print $line1_answers[2];
 93.  print "\n<P>\n";
 94.  print "What is your favorite fruit?:\n<BR>\n";
 95.  print "Apple: ";
 96.  print $line2_answers[0];
 97.  print "<BR>\n";
 98.  print "Orange: ";
 99.  print $line2_answers[1];
100.  print "\n<P>\n";
101.  print "I use the Internet:\n<BR>\n";
102.  print "0-5 hours per week: ";
103.  print $line3_answers[0];
104.  print "<BR>\n";
105.  print "6-10 hours per week: ";
106.  print $line3_answers[1];
107.  print "<BR>\n";
108.  print "11+ hours per week: ";
109.  print $line3_answers[2];
110.  print "\n<P>\n";
111.  print <<EOF;
112.  </BODY>
113.  </HTML>
114.  EOF
```

HOW THE SCRIPT WORKS

5. This command (-e) does a conditional if to see if poll.dat exists. If poll.dat is not found, then it will be created and initialized with values set at 0.

6–8. poll.dat is opened—the FILEHANDLE POLL is used.

9–12. Next, loop through the contents of the file and place them in the @poll array. (If the file does not exist, then the FILEHANDLE didn't get opened; lines 9–12 will not get executed, resulting in the @poll array not existing, being empty.)

14. Arrange an array with elements numbering 1 through 3. Next, loop through all these elements.

17. Create the $this_line variable, by appending each element to the string line. So, the first loop through, $this_line will equal line1, the second time through, it will contain line2, and so on.

18. Assign element 0 of the `@poll` array to `$line1`, element 1 to `$line2`, and so on. (Since `$this_line` equals `line1` on the first pass, `$$this_line` is the equivalent to `$line1`.)

14–20. What if `poll.dat` does not exist? Well, as you saw earlier, if this is so, then `@poll` doesn't exist. Since `@poll` doesn't exist, `$line1` will be empty, as will `$line2` and `$line3`. Now take a look at poll.html. The first question has three answers. This question is associated with `$line1`. If `$line1` is empty, then three 0s, separated by tabs, get assigned to it (this is the format of poll.dat, which you will see a little later). The same thing is done for lines 2 and 3 (notice that `$line2` only gets two 0s, because there are only two answers to Question #2, whereas Questions #1 and #3 have three answers each). The layout of poll.dat will be three lines, since there are three questions, with each line having the number of answers to each question separated by tabs. Here is a possible example of the contents of poll.dat:

Blue	Red	Other
3	3	4
4	6	
3	3	4

Three people chose Blue as their favorite color, three people chose Red, and four people chose Other.

36–67. Add 1 to the appropriate counter depending on which option was chosen on each question.

38–72. Assemble the updated poll.dat, and end the script.

73–114. Print out the return page, which displays the number of answers to each question.

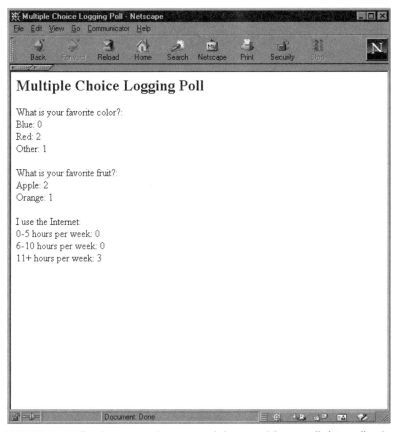

FIGURE 3–4 All values are written to and then read from poll.dat. poll.cgi then displays this HTML page with the appended values.

◆ Project III: Quiz

Files Used	Permissions
quiz.html	644
quiz.cgi	755

Here is a pretty straightforward script that tests the values of the questions inside the script itself. If an answer is tested to be true, it is printed in bold. If the answer is tested to be false, it is printed in red.

HTML 3–4
quiz.html

```
<HTML>
<HEAD>
<TITLE>
Quiz
</TITLE>
</HEAD>
<BODY BGCOLOR="#FFFFFF">
<H2>Multiple Choice Questionnaire</H2>
<P>
<FORM ACTION="quiz.cgi" METHOD="POST">
How many states are there in the US?:
<BR>
<INPUT TYPE="RADIO" NAME="STATES" VALUE="50">50
<BR>
<INPUT TYPE="RADIO" NAME="STATES" VALUE="51">51
<BR>
<INPUT TYPE="RADIO" NAME="STATES" VALUE="1">1
<P>
People need what to survive?:
<BR>
<INPUT TYPE="RADIO" NAME="SURVIVE" VALUE="Air">Air
<BR>
<INPUT TYPE="RADIO" NAME="SURVIVE" VALUE="Donuts">Donuts
<BR>
<INPUT TYPE="RADIO" NAME="SURVIVE" VALUE="Pez">Pez
<P>
Stitch Magazine is a great magazine.:
<BR>
<INPUT TYPE="RADIO" NAME="STITCH" VALUE="True">True
<BR>
<INPUT TYPE="RADIO" NAME="STITCH" VALUE="False">False
<P>
The Moon is made of cheese.:
<BR>
<INPUT TYPE="RADIO" NAME="MOON" VALUE="True">True
<BR>
<INPUT TYPE="RADIO" NAME="MOON" VALUE="False">False
<P>
2 + 2 is what?:
<BR>
<INPUT TYPE="RADIO" NAME="ADD" VALUE="0">0
<BR>
<INPUT TYPE="RADIO" NAME="ADD" VALUE="4">4
<BR>
<INPUT TYPE="RADIO" NAME="ADD" VALUE="My I.Q.">My I.Q.
```

```
<P>
<INPUT TYPE="SUBMIT" VALUE="Submit">
</FORM>
</BODY>
</HTML>
```

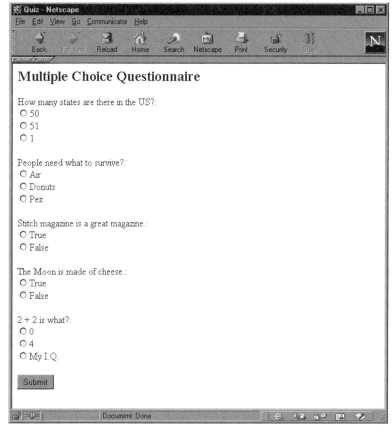

FIGURE 3–5 Interface of the quiz script

Script 3–4
quiz.cgi

```
1.  #!/usr/bin/perl
2.  require "get_form_data.pl";
3.  &get_form_data;
4.  print "Content-type: text/html\n\n";
5.  print <<EOF;
```

```
6.   <HTML>
7.   <HEAD>
8.   <TITLE>
9.   Multiple Choice Questionnaire
10.  </TITLE>
11.  </HEAD>
12.  <BODY BGCOLOR="#FFFFFF">
13.  <H2>Multiple Choice Logging Poll</H2>
14.  <P>
15.  How many states are there in the US?:
16.  <BR>
17.  EOF
18.  if($FORM{'STATES'} eq "50")
19.  {
20.     print "<B>50</B>";
21.  }
22.  else
23.  {
24.     print "50";
25.  }
26.  print "\n<BR>\n";
27.  if($FORM{'STATES'} eq "51")
28.  {
29.     print "<FONT COLOR=\"RED\"><B>51</B></FONT>";
30.  }
31.  else
32.  {
33.     print "51";
34.  }
35.  print "\n<BR>\n";
36.  if($FORM{'STATES'} eq "1")
37.  {
38.     print "<FONT COLOR=\"RED\">1</FONT>";
39.  }
40.  else
41.  {
42.     print "1";
43.  }
44.  print "\n<P>\n";
45.  print "People need what to survive?:\n<BR>\n";
46.  if($FORM{'SURVIVE'} eq "Air")
47.  {
48.     print "<B>Air</B>";
49.  }
50.  else
51.  {
52.     print "Air";
53.  }
54.  print "<BR>\n";
```

```
55.  if($FORM{'SURVIVE'} eq "Donuts")
56.  {
57.     print "<FONT COLOR=\"RED\">Donuts</FONT>";
58.  }
59.  else
60.  {
61.     print "Donuts";
62.  }
63.  print "<BR>\n";
64.  if($FORM{'SURVIVE'} eq "Pez")
65.  {
66.     print "<FONT COLOR=\"RED\">Pez</FONT>";
67.  }
68.  else
69.  {
70.     print "Pez";
71.  }
72.  print "\n<P>\n";
73.  print "Stitch Magazine is a great magazine.:\n<BR>\n";
74.  if($FORM{'STITCH'} eq "True")
75.  {
76.     print "<B>True</B>";
77.  }
78.  else
79.  {
80.     print "True";
81.  }
82.  print "<BR>\n";
83.  if($FORM{'STITCH'} eq "False")
84.  {
85.     print "<FONT COLOR=\"RED\">False</FONT>";
86.  }
87.  else
88.  {
89.     print "False";
90.  }
91.  print "\n<P>\n";
92.  print "The Moon is made of cheese.:\n<BR>\n";
93.  if($FORM{'MOON'} eq "True")
94.  {
95.     print "<FONT COLOR=\"RED\">True</FONT>";
96.  }
97.  else
98.  {
99.     print "<B>True</B>";
100. }
101. print "<BR>\n";
102. if($FORM{'MOON'} eq "False")
103. {
```

```
104.    print "<B>False</B>";
105. }
106. else
107. {
108.    print "False";
109. }
110. print "\n<P>\n";
111. print "2 + 2 is what?:\n<BR>\n";
112. if($FORM{'ADD'} eq "0")
113. {
114.    print "<FONT COLOR=\"RED\">0</FONT>";
115. }
116. else
117. {
118.    print "0";
119. }
120. print "<BR>\n";
121. if($FORM{'ADD'} eq "4")
122. {
123.    print "<B>4</B>";
124. }
125. else
126. {
127.    print "4";
128. }
129. print "<BR>\n";
130. if($FORM{'ADD'} eq "My I.Q.")
131. {
132.    print "<FONT COLOR=\"RED\">My I.Q.</FONT>";
133. }
134. else
135. {
136.    print "My I.Q.";
137. }
138. print "\n<P>\n";
139. print <<EOF;
140. </BODY>
141. </HTML>
142. EOF
143. exit;
```

HOW THE SCRIPT WORKS

2–3. Begin by getting the form data.

4. The script starts formatting the return.

18–25. The correct answer to Question #1 is 50. Now the script tests what the value of STATES is with eq. If the person entered 50 for that question, then the answer is printed out in bold (`<B>50</B>`), indicating this was the correct answer. Otherwise, (`else`), the user didn't enter 50 for this question, so a nonbold 50 is printed out.

27–34. Check to see if the user chose 51 for the first question. If so, 51 is printed in bold red, indicating a wrong answer. Otherwise, we simply print out the second option.

36–43. Do the same thing for the third option. The rest of the script follows suit, doing the same tests for the other four questions (`SURVIVE`, `STITCH`, `MOON`, and `ADD`).

140–141. The script is ended by closing the `BODY` and `HTML` tags.

143. Exit the script.

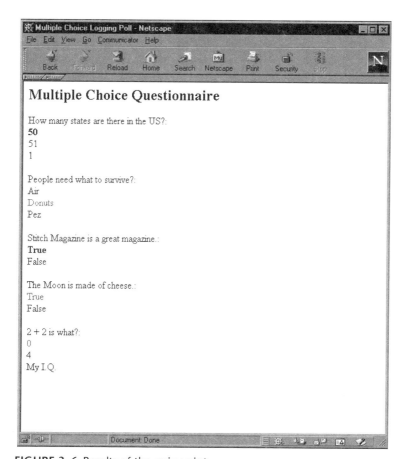

FIGURE 3–6 Results of the quiz script

RECAP

This was a long chapter! You learned how to:

- Append to an HTML file to build a simple guestbook.
- Write scores to an external file to keep track of how many people voted for a particular category.
- Evaluate answers to questions to serve an answer page showing which were correct and which were not.

ADVANCED PROJECTS

Modify poll.cgi to enable file locking, which we discussed in Chapter 2. Right now, the poll.dat file is wide open to be written to by multiple people because poll.cgi does not lock it when opening.

4 Searching the Web

IN THIS CHAPTER

- Project I: Basic Search Engine
- Project II: Advanced Search Engine
- Recap
- Advanced Projects

After a period of time, most personal or corporate Web sites grow very large, so large in fact that their users will have a hard time finding all the appropriate documents. Besides setting up an enormous site map, which might end up being too cumbersome for a user to search through anyway, the best solution is to set up a search engine.

Search engines vary in complexity and functionality. For your site, you probably don't need to set up a highly complex search engine such as HotBot or Infoseek; therefore, in this chapter, you will learn how to build a search engine to search on content found within the local directory. As the scripts find the keyword(s) that the user enters, it will display that page on a list by its <TITLE></TITLE> *name. In the case of Shelley Biotechnologies, the new company that you will be working with for the remainder of this book, you will start off with a few product pages. If a user wants to search on a Brain Regenerator, then it is a good idea to have the name somewhere in the* <TITLE></TITLE> *tags so when it is listed from the search it will be evident that it is a product. This isn't necessary for the script to work because the script will search on all content in the pages. This is just a good idea for listing purposes.*

The search.cgi will search through a single directory based on the keywords the user enters in the search field. First, you will need to create a few HTML pages to perform this search on some titles. Start with the following three pages and feel free to add as many as you want to have more of a selection.

◆ Project I: Basic Search Engine

Files Used	Permissions
page1.html	644
page2.html	644
page3.html	644
search.cgi	744

HTML 4–1
page1.html

```
<HTML>
<HEAD>
<TITLE>DNA Compiler</TITLE>
</HEAD>
<BODY BGCOLOR="#FFFFFF">
This is an HTML page for the DNA Compiler.
</BODY>
</HTML>
```

HTML 4–2
page2.html

```
<HTML>
<HEAD>
<TITLE>Cloning Kit 2000</TITLE>
</HEAD>
<BODY BGCOLOR="#FFFFFF">
This is an HTML page for the Cloning Kit 2000.<BR>
```

```
</BODY>
</HTML>
```

HTML 4–3
page3.html

```
<HTML>
<HEAD>
<TITLE>Brain Regenerator</TITLE>
</HEAD>
<BODY BGCOLOR="#FFFFFF">
This is an HTML page for the Brain Regenerator.
</BODY>
</HTML>
```

Next, create a form in which the user can enter keywords. Remember that this is searching only in the local directory, so be sure to have search.html as well as the previous three HTML documents in the same directory so search.cgi can perform its search successfully (see Figure 4–1).

HTML 4–4
search.html

```
<HTML>
<HEAD>
<TITLE>Search</TITLE>
</HEAD>
<BODY BGCOLOR="#FFFFFF">
<FORM ACTION="search.cgi" METHOD="POST">
   <INPUT TYPE="TEXT" NAME="search">
   <P>
   <INPUT TYPE="SUBMIT" VALUE="Search">
</FORM>
</BODY>
</HTML>
```

NEW FEATURES

Regular Expressions

Regular expressions are a powerful tool used in Perl. A regular expression is a pattern to be matched against any string. Matching a regular expression against a string either succeeds or fails. Usually, this success or failure is all the script cares about. Other times, you may want to replace a certain string with another string such as a search and replace. In

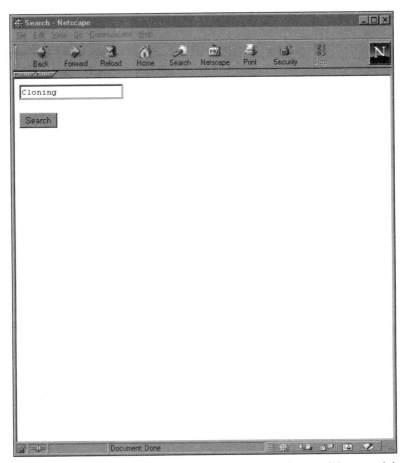

FIGURE 4–1 Interface for search engine. User will input keyword(s) to search by.

Perl, regular expressions are expressed by surrounding the string to be matched in forward slashes (/).

```
if(/something/)
{
    print "we found something in $_\n";
}
```

You may ask, "What are we testing the regular expression against?" Here, the special $_ variable comes into play. When a target is not specified (more on how to specify a target later), any regular expression is performed on $_. In this example, if `$_` contains the string something, then it is printed out that it has been found.

What if you want to replace a certain string with another string? Instead of just putting slashes around our regular expression, the letter s (substitution) is placed in front of the first slash, followed by the pattern to be matched, then another slash to separate the two, then the pattern with which to replace the first pattern, and finally, another slash.

```
s/something/something else/g;
```

The preceding line replaces the string something with something else in `$_`.

NOTE

The =~ character tests to see if both sides are true, in the same way you used == earlier, only =~ is used to test regular expressions.

!= does the exact opposite by testing to see if both sides are not equal to each other. If they are not, then this will result in true.

What if you want to perform a regular expression search and replace on a variable other than `$_`? This is where the =~ operator is used. Just as we did earlier, you may only be interested in whether or not the regular expression succeeded. Either way, the syntax for the regular expression is the same, you will just use it like this:

```
if($something =~ /something/)
{
    print "we found something \n";
}
```

If `$something` contains the text something, again, it is simply printed out that it has been found.

```
$something =~ s/something/something else/;
```

Now replace any and all occurrences of something with something else in `$something`.

More on regular expressions in Chapter 5, "Who's Watching Whom."

Now that you have all of the HTML out of the way, it's time to set up the script that will be doing all the work. You'll remember from Chapter 3 that all future script will be using the `require` function to require the file `get_form_data.pl` that you created in Chapter 2, as search.cgi will be making a call to it on lines 2 and 3.

Script 4–1
search.cgi

```perl
1.  #!/usr/bin/perl
2.  require "get_form_data.pl";
3.  &get_form_data();
4.  $search_term = $FORM{'search'};
5.  print "Content-type: text/html\n\n";
6.  opendir(DIR, ".");
7.  while($file = readdir(DIR))
8.  {
9.      next if($file !~ /.html/);
10.     open(FILE, $file);
11.     $found_match = 0;
12.     $title = "";
13.     while(<FILE>)
14.     {
15.         if(/$search_term/i)
16.         {
17.             $found_match = 1;
18.         }
19.         if(/<TITLE>/)
20.         {
21.             chop;
22.             $title = $_;
23.             $title =~ s/<TITLE>//g;
24.             $title =~ s/<\/TITLE>//g;
25.         }
26.     }
27.     if($title eq "")
28.     {
29.         $title = $file;
30.     }
31.     if($found_match)
32.     {
33.         print "<A HREF=\"$file\">$title</A>\n";
34.         print "<BR>\n";
35.     }
36.     close(FILE);
37. }
38. closedir(DIR);
39. exit;
```

HOW THE SCRIPT WORKS

4. First, the variable $search_term is created, which contains the keyword(s) the user submitted.

6. Open the current directory for reading, using the opendir command.

7–35. Loop through every single file and directory in the directory that was just opened in line 6.

9. The next command skips the current iteration of the loop in which it is contained, and moves on to the next. If it is at the last iteration, the loop simply ends. Here the current iteration of the loop is skipped only if the file being looked at does not contain .htm, using regular expressions. This line uses the !~ operator to perform a regular expression match on whatever is put in // (in this case, .html). The !~ operator is the exact opposite of the =~ operator, which, in this case, will only skip the current iteration of the loop if the current file *does* contain .html.

10. Once an HTML file has been found, it is opened.

11–12. Some temporary variables that will be explained later.

13–26. Loop through the HTML file.

15–18. This line uses regular expressions to see if the current line contains the keyword the user entered. Notice that the =~ or !~ operators weren't used. Since the variable that contains the current line is $_, we don't need to use them. When a regular expression is enclosed in slashes, the $_ is tested for the text inside the slashes. The =~ and !~ operators are for testing a variable other than $_ against the regular expression. Also notice the single letter i after the second slash. This says to perform a case insensitive match. If we omit this, then the keyword must match *exactly*. Now, suppose a match is found, then the $found_match variable is set to 1, to be used in lines 27–31.

19–25. Now the current line is tested to see if it contains <TITLE>. This will be used to determine what text will be displayed for the hyperlink to the matched page. These lines only work in the intended way if the title appears in between <TITLE> and </TITLE>, all on the same line.

21. Remove the newline from the $_ variable. chop(); operates on $_ if a target isn't specified in parentheses.

23–24. Using regular expressions, remove <TITLE> and </TITLE> from the $title variable we just defined in line 22. This regular expression uses substitution to remove the text. The syntax of this is s/old text/new text/; This will replace old text with new text. Since the goal is to completely remove the old text, nothing is put between the last set of slashes.

27–30. In case a title is not found, or the HTML page doesn't have the opening and closing tags on the same line, set the $title variable to the name of the file so that the hyperlink is displayed.

31–35. If a match is found in the current file, print out a hyperlink to it, using the $title variable that was just assembled, for the descriptive text displayed to the user.

36–39. Finally, close the FILEHANDLE at the end of each iteration (thus closing each file once the script is finished with it).

◆ Project II: Advanced Search Engine

Files Used	Permissions
search2.cgi	744

The search.cgi script showed you how to search through all the HTML files in the current directory by keywords. With the following script, script2.cgi, you will be able to search through all the files in the current directory, as well as search in subdirectories beyond that recursively.

For this project, you should set up several directories embedded within other directories at least three levels deep, with names such as directory_1, directory_2, and directory_3 all within each other. Use the same HTML files that were used in the last project, appending the directory names to the end of the titles and body. For example:

```
<HTML>
<HEAD>
<TITLE>DNA Compiler - Directory 1</TITLE>
</HEAD>
<BODY BGCOLOR="#FFFFFF">
This is an HTML page for the DNA Compiler. - Directory 1
</BODY>
</HTML>
```

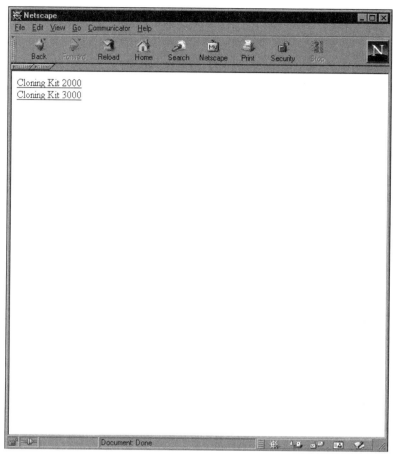

FIGURE 4–2 Results of the search listed by <TITLE> with links to the appropriate pages in the current directory

Change Directory 1 to the appropriate number of the directory you are in. This will be a quick way to see that the script has searched and listed the HTML files from these directories.

NEW FEATURES

local

Up to now the variables you have used have been global throughout the entire program. Sometimes, however, when using these variables you would like to make a variable's value only valid for a certain subroutine. Then once the subroutine is exited, the variable returns to its old value.

```perl
#!/usr/bin/perl
$number = 5;
print "\$number is equal to: $number\n";
&new_routine;
sub new_routine
{
   local ($number);
   $number = 10;
   print "Inside local, \$number is equal to: $number\n";
}
print "\$number is now equal to: $number\n\n";
```

Results

```
$number is equal to: 5
Inside local, $number is equal to: 10
$number is now equal to: 5
```

foreach

The `foreach` function is another one of the looping functions. It is used when sorting through an array, where it will start with the first element in the array and perform whatever statement it has after it on the element. When finished with the statements, the second element in the array will be selected and the process begins again until all elements in the array have been looped through.

```perl
#!/usr/bin/perl
@count = ('1', '2', '3', '4', '5');
print "I can count to: \n";
foreach $count (@count)
{
   print $count, "\n";
}
```

Results

```
I can count to:
1
2
3
4
5
```

Script 4–2
search2.cgi

1. `#!/usr/bin/perl`
2. `require "get_form_data.pl";`
3. `&get_form_data();`

```perl
4.  $search_term = $FORM{'search'};
5.  print "Content-type: text/html\n\n";
6.  &search(".");
7.  print <<EOF;
8.  <HTML>
9.  <HEAD>
10. <TITLE>
11. Search
12. </TITLE>
13. </HEAD>
14. <BODY BGCOLOR="#FFFFFF">
15. EOF
16. foreach $file (@found_set)
17. {
18.     print "<A HREF=\"$file\">$Title{$file}</A>\n";
19.     print "<BR>\n";
20. }
21. print <<EOF;
22. </BODY>
23. </HTML>
24. EOF
25. exit;
26. sub search
27. {
28.     local ($dir) = @_;
29.     if($dir eq ".")
30.     {
31.         opendir(DIR, ".");
32.         $dir = "";
33.     }
34.     else
35.     {
36.         opendir(DIR, $dir);
37.         $dir .= "/";
38.     }
39.     foreach $file (sort readdir(DIR))
40.     {
41.         next if($file eq "." || $file eq "..");
42.         $file = $dir . $file;
43.         next if(($file !~ /.htm/) && (!(-d $file)));
44.
45.         if(-d $file)
46.         {
47.             &search($file);
48.             next;
49.         }
50.         open(FILE, $file);
51.         $found_match = 0;
52.         $title = "";
```

```
53.        while(<FILE>)
54.        {
55.            if(/$search_term/i)
56.            {
57.                $found_match = 1;
58.            }
59.            if(/<TITLE>/)
60.            {
61.                chop;
62.                $title = $_;
63.                $title =~ s/<TITLE>//g;
64.                $title =~ s/<\/TITLE>//g;
65.            }
66.        }
67.        if($found_match)
68.        {
69.            push(@found_set, $file);
70.            if($title eq "")
71.            {
72.                $Title{$file} = $file;
73.            }
74.            else
75.            {
76.                $Title{$file} = $title;
77.            }
78.        }
79.        close(FILE);
80.        print "<P>\n";
81.    }
82.    closedir(DIR);
83. }
```

HOW THE SCRIPT WORKS

6. Call the subroutine `search`, which begins at line 26, passing it the directory that will be used to begin searching. Use "`.`" to indicate to start at the current directory. The arguments that are passed to the subroutine are then put into the `@_` array. So, the first argument is in `$_[0]`, the second in `$_[1]`, and so forth.

7–15. Print out header HTML.

16–20. After execution of the subroutine is finished, an array is assembled along with an associative array with the filename and title of the matching HTML pages that were found. Now the script simply prints out the HREF tags to them.

21–25. Print out footer HTML and exit.

26. Define the `search` subroutine.

28. Here the `local` command is used to define the variable that contains the directory passed to the subroutine. Using `local` makes this definition local to this calling of the subroutine only, so if the subroutine is called again later, another value can be passed into the `$dir` variable, but it won't overwrite the first one.

29–38. Here the directory passed to the subroutine is opened. Now `$dir` needs to be set to `""`, only if it is searching on `"."`, and otherwise, appending `"/"` to `$dir`, so that the pointer to the matched file points to the right place.

39–75. Loop through each file and directory sorted alphabetically.

41–43. Skip the `"."` and `".."` directories, as well as files that don't contain `.htm`. The files that contain `.htm` can't be ignored, since you will want to see directories, too.

45–49. If the current item being looked at is a directory, call `search` on it. This is where the recursion occurs. Once the script is done traversing this directory (and any other directories contained in that directory), the script returns to line 29, which skips to the next iteration.

50–52. Once an HTML file has been found, it is opened. Some temp files are created that will be explained later.

53–66. Loop through each line in the file, since by now it can't be a directory, and it contains `.htm`, so it must be an HTML file. This block is unchanged from search.cgi.

67–73. If a match in this file is found, then the name of the file is *pushed* (which by now contains the full path from the current directory) onto the `@pushed_set` array. The title of the HTML page is added to the `%Title` associative array, keyed on the name of the file.

74–78. Close the FILEHANDLE, print out a paragraph tag, then once the files are looped through, close the directory handle, and, finally, the subroutine.

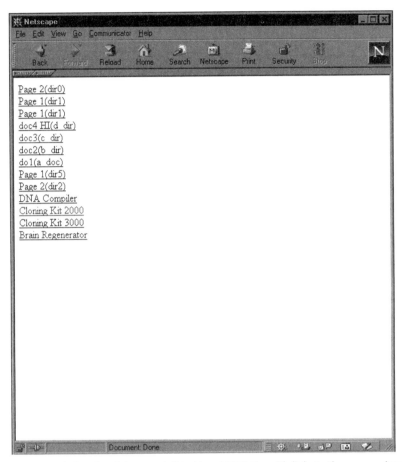

FIGURE 4–3 Results of the search listed by <TITLE> with links to the appropriate pages in the current directory, as well as all subdirectories

RECAP

Using regular expressions is a very powerful feature that Perl has to offer, as you have by now undoubtedly noticed. Within these last two scripts, especially in Project II, you have learned the basics of building a very robust search engine.

ADVANCED PROJECTS

Currently, the search.cgi and search2.cgi scripts will only list HTML files that have the <TITLE>Some Title</TITLE> tags on one line. If an HTML page is set up like this:

```
<TITLE>
Some Title
</TITLE>
```

then the page would not be listed. Go back and correct this problem so that it will account for both ways of having the <TITLE> tags set up.

5 Who's Watching Whom

IN THIS CHAPTER

- Project I: Tracking Visitors
- Project II: Password Protection
- Recap
- Advanced Projects

Throughout all the scripts you have worked with in this book, you probably didn't even stop to think that there is a whole other world of CGI lying just below the surface watching who you are, where you came from, and what browser you're using, among many other things. OK, so maybe we're being a little dramatic, but it was a fun way to open you to the world of environment variables.

Environment variables are sets of data that are sent from your browser to the Web server every time you connect to it. Depending on the server or the browser, your mileage may vary, but for the most part the types of information passed are the client's IP address, browser type, and type of operating system. Information about the server is also passed along, such as the type of Web server, the version number, and the server administrator contact.

Script 5–1 is a little script to pull and display all the environment variables. It uses a special variable called the %ENV, *which is another type of array called an associative array (which you will learn about a little later in the chapter). Once you have env_var.cgi script on your system, simply run it from your browser and you will see something like Figure 5–1.*

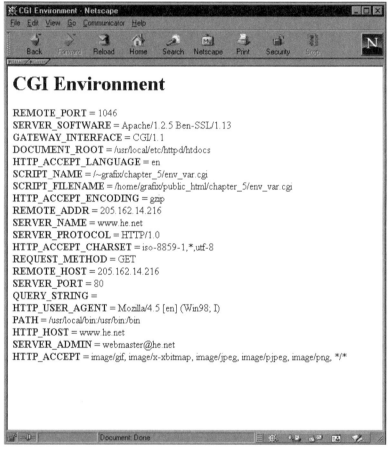

FIGURE 5–1 A display of the Web server and the client/server environment variables

Script 5–1
env_var.cgi

```perl
1.  #!/usr/bin/perl
2.  print "Content-type: text/html\n\n";
3.  print "<HTML>\n";
```

```
 4.  print "<HEAD>\n";
 5.  print "<TITLE>CGI Environment</TITLE>\n";
 6.  print "</HEAD>\n";
 7.  print "<BODY>\n";
 8.  print "<H1>CGI Environment</H1>\n";
 9.  foreach $env_var (keys %ENV)
10.  {
11.     print "<B>$env_var</B> =
12.     $ENV{$env_var}<BR>\n";
13.  }
14.  print "</BODY>\n";
15.  print "</HTML>\n";
```

HOW THE SCRIPT WORKS

9. Start looping through all the keys in the associative array %ENV.

11. Here we print out the key, which is the identifier for each value.

12. Now print out the value for that key.

◆ Project I: Tracking Visitors

Files Used	Permissions
env_var.cgi	755
save.cgi	755
view.cgi	755

After all your hard work building your company's Web site you might be wondering, "How do I know if this site is generating any traffic?" Script 5–2 provides an effective way to track some of the information that is pulled from the client/server environment variables when they visit your site.

When a user's browser opens save.cgi, a couple of pieces of data are stored from the environment variables:

HTTP_USER_AGENT.

Gathers the browser type and version as well as the operating system.

REMOTE_ADDR.

Gathers the IP address of the user.

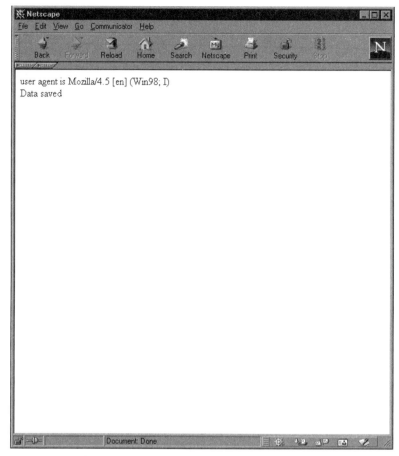

FIGURE 5–2 When the save.cgi script is executed, these variables are logged to the client_log.txt file

NEW FEATURES

Associative Arrays

An associative array (also called a *hash*) is a lot like a normal array in that it is a collection of scalar values, each selected by some index value. The difference is that this index value can be any scalar, not just an integer. These scalars are called *keys* and are used to call the values from the array.

The individual elements of an associative array are not arranged in any particular order. Perl stores the values in its own internal order, which makes it easier for Perl to find the matching value without examining every single element.

Remember that we refer to an array with @. With associative arrays, we use % instead. Just like regular arrays, when accessing individual elements we use $, only instead of using square brackets ([ ]), we use curly ones ({ }). The key, which was mentioned earlier, appears in between the brackets. This key can either be explicitly declared, or we can use a variable to represent it.

printf

The printf operator is used for printing out formatted text. It takes a list of arguments just like print. The first argument is a format control string, which defines how to print out the remaining arguments. Following this control string are the variable(s) that will be printed out. Consider the following example:

```
printf "%5s %5.2f %15d", $a, $b, $c;
```

This line prints out $a as a 5-character field (the s after the 5 stands for string), followed by a space, then $b as a floating point value with two decimal places in a 5-character field, then another space, followed by $c as a 15-character decimal integer.

view.cgi is used to display all of the information that save.cgi has just saved to the logfile.txt file. If you look at the logfile.txt file you will notice all of the IP addresses that accessed the save.cgi file.

Script 5–2
save.cgi

```
1.   #!/usr/bin/perl
2.   print "Content-type: text/html\n\n";
3.   $logfile = "client_log.txt";
4.   &get_data;
5.   &save_data;
6.   &print_return_page;
7.   exit;

8.   sub get_data
9.   {
10.     $user_agent = $ENV{'HTTP_USER_AGENT'};

11.     # get the Browser Version
12.     ($Browser_Version) = split(" ", $user_agent);
13.     ($Type, $Version) = split("\/", $Browser_Version);

14.     # get the Browser Type
```

```
15.    if($user_agent =~ /Nav/)
16.    {
17.       $Browser_Type = "Netscape Navigator $Version";
18.    } elsif($user_agent =~ /MSIE/)
19.    {
20.       $Browser_Type = "Microsoft Internet Explorer
          $Version";
21.    } elsif($user_agent =~ /Lynx/)
22.    {
23.       $Browser_Type = "Lynx $Version";
24.    }
25.    else
26.    {
27.       $Browser_Type = "Other";
28.    }

29.    # assemble the date
30.    ($sec, $min, $hour, $mday, $mon, $year, $wday, $yday,
       $isdst) = localtime(time);
31.    $date = $mon+1 . "/" . $mday . "/" . $year;

32.    # get the OS
33.    if($user_agent =~ /Win95/)
34.    {
35.       $Operating_System = "Windows 9x";
36.    } elsif($user_agent =~ /Windows 95/)
37.    {
38.       $Operating_System = "Windows 95";
39.    } elsif($user_agent =~ /Windows 98/)
40.    {
41.       $Operating_System = "Windows 98";
42.    } elsif($user_agent =~ /WinNT/)
43.    {
44.       $Operating_System = "Windows NT";
45.    } elsif($user_agent =~ /Mac/)
46.    {
47.       $Operating_System = "Macintosh";
48.    } else
49.    {
50.       $Operating_System = "Other";
51.    }

52.    # get the users' IP
53.    $Remote_Address = $ENV{'REMOTE_ADDR'};
54. }

55. sub save_data
56. {
57.    open(LOGFILE, ">>$logfile");
```

```
58.    print LOGFILE $date . "\t" . $Operating_System . "\t"
       . $Browser_Type . "\t" . $Remote_Address . "\n";
59.    close(LOGFILE);
60. }

61. sub print_return_page
62. {
63.    print <<EOF;
64.    <HTML>
65.    <BODY BGCOLOR="#FFFFFF">
66.    Data saved
67.    </BODY>
68.    </HTML>
69.    EOF
70. }
```

HOW THE SCRIPT WORKS

3. Define the name of the file in which we will store the data.

4–6. Call the subroutines that get the data, save it to the logfile, and then print an HTML page.

8–63. Here we define the `get_data` subroutine. In this subroutine we will analyze the data from the client environment variables, saving what we need into our own variables to save into the logfile later.

10. The client browser stores information about itself in `$ENV{'HTTP_USER_AGENT'}` and sends this information to the Web server every time it requests a document.

12–13. Take a look at env_var.cgi. Knowing how the user agent information is going to look, we can extract the name and version of the browser using these two lines, using `split`.

15–28. Here we use regular expressions to check if `$user_agent` contains any number of certain text strings, and depending on which one, we define our browser type accordingly.

30–31. Now we assemble the date using the `localtime` function. The `localtime` function always returns an array of nine elements, in a certain order. Here we simply place those elements into descriptively named variables, then define our `$date` variable using the month, day, and year (we add 1 to `$mon` because `localtime` stores the month from 0–11).

33–51. Now we determine the operating system based on whether or not `$user_agent` contains one of several different text strings, just as before.

53. Get the IP address of the client machine.

55–60. Start the subroutine that saves the data we got from `&get_data`.

57. Open `$logfile` (which we defined in line 3) for appending to. (Note that the logfile will have to be either group writable and be assigned to the same group as the Web server process, or else it must be world writable. Otherwise, the Web server will not have permission to write to it.)

58–59. Print out the data we assembled in `&get_data` to the logfile, then close the FILEHANDLE.

61–70. Finally, define `&print_return_page`, which prints out a message to the client that their data was saved.

Script 5–3
view.cgi

```
1.  #!/usr/bin/perl
2.  print "Content-type: text/html\n\n";
3.  &get_logfile_data;
4.  &print_header;
5.  &print_data;
6.  &print_footer;

7.  sub get_logfile_data
8.  {
9.      $logfile = "client_log.txt";
10.     open(LOGFILE, $logfile);
11.     $number_of_accesses = 0;
12.     while(<LOGFILE>)
13.     {
14.         # print LOGFILE $date . "\t" . $Operating_System .
            "\t" . $Browser_Type . " " . 14. $Version . "\t" .
            $Remote_Address . "\n";
15.         chop;
16.         ($log_date, $log_Operating_System, $log_Browser,
            $log_Remote_Address) = split("\t", $_);
17.         $Date{$log_date}++;
18.         $OS{$log_Operating_System}++;
19.         $Browser{$log_Browser}++;
```

```
20.        $Remote_Address{$log_Remote_Address} =
           $log_Remote_Address;
21.        $number_of_accesses++;
22.     }
23.  }

24.  sub print_header
25.  {
26.     print <<EOF;
27.     <HTML>
28.     <BODY BGCOLOR="#FFFFFF">
29.     EOF
30.  }

31.  sub print_data
32.  {
33.     print "<B><FONT SIZE=\"+1\">Number of 34. Accesses on
        each Date:</FONT></B><BR>\n";
34.     foreach $each_date (sort keys %Date)
35.     {
36.        $percentage_dates = ($Date{$each_date} /
           $number_of_accesses) * 100;
37.        print "$each_date: <B>$Date{$each_date}</B> ";
38.        printf("(%.2f%)", $percentage_dates);
39.        print "<BR>\n";
40.     }
41.     print "<P>\n";
42.     print "<B><FONT SIZE=\"+1\">Operating Systems:</
        FONT></B><BR>\n";
43.     foreach $each_OS (sort keys %OS)
44.     {
45.        $percentage_OS = ($OS{$each_OS} /
           $number_of_accesses) * 100;
46.        print "$each_OS: <B>$OS{$each_OS}</B> ";
47.        printf("(%.2f%)", $percentage_OS);
48.        print "<BR>\n";
49.     }
50.     print "<P>\n";
51.     print "<B><FONT SIZE=\"+1\">Browsers:</FONT></B><BR>\n";
52.     foreach $each_Browser (sort keys %Browser)
53.     {
54.        $percentage_Browser = ($Browser{$each_Browser} /
           $number_of_accesses) * 100;
55.        print "$each_Browser: <B>$Browser{$each_Browser}</
           B> ";
56.        printf("(%.2f%)", $percentage_Browser);
57.        print "<BR>\n";
58.     }
59.     print "<P>\n";
```

```
60.    $num_unique_ips = scalar keys %Remote_Address;
61.    print "Number of unique IP's: <B>$num_unique_ips</B>\n";
62.  }

63.  sub print_footer
64.  {
65.     print <<EOF;
66.     </BODY>
67.     </HTML>
68.     EOF
69.  }
```

HOW THE SCRIPT WORKS

3. The &get_logfile_data subroutine opens the logfile and saves the data from it into a number of associative arrays.

4. &print_header prints out header HTML text.

5. &print_data takes the data from the associative arrays we created in &get_logfile_data and displays it in a readable format.

6. &print_footer prints out footer HTML text.

9. Here again we define the logfile from which we will be reading.

10. Open the logfile for reading.

11. We want to know how many accesses we had, so we initialize $number_of_accesses.

12–21. Loop through the contents of the logfile.

14. Remove the carriage return from $_ (remember that while in a loop like this, each line is stored in $_ during each iteration of the loop).

15. Using split, extract the different data entries from $_ (the current line in the logfile).

16. Here we are using associative arrays. We add 1 to $Date{$log_date}. If this variable does not exist, Perl simply treats it as if it is 0, and adds 1 to it. Since $log_date is the date stored in the logfile, each time we come across this same date, we will add 1 to it, thus counting the number of accesses for that date.

17–18. The same thing is done for the operating system and browser.

19. Store the IP address of the client machine in `%Remote_Address`. Since no associative array can have two keys that are named alike, we can be assured that the number of keys in `%Remote_Address` is the number of unique IPs that accessed our page.

20. Add 1 to the number of accesses we have gotten so far.

30–61. Print out the data we assembled in `&get_logfile_data`.

33–39. Loop through each date in `%Date`, sorted based on the key (so the earliest date comes first).

35. Define the percentage of accesses this date received.

37. We use the `printf` command to format the percentage so that only the first two numbers after the decimal point appear (`.4f` instead of `.2f` would make the first four numbers after the decimal appear instead).

40–57. Do the same thing as in lines 33–39 for the operating system and browser.

49. Here we get the number of keys contained in `%Remote_Address`. `scalar keys %Remote_Address` returns the keys of `%Remote_Address` in a scalar context. In this case, the number of keys contained in it. (Nonscalar context would just be an array of all the keys in the associative array. This is why we use `foreach` to loop through all the keys in an associative array.)

You could have save.cgi linked to a page and then have the script auto-refresh to the next page, or you could use the Server Side Includes (SSI) function.

NEW FEATURES

Server Side Includes (SSI)

SSI files are HTML files that can access other files and build their pages into their own. What you will use it for here is for a user to access an HTML file called logme.html so that when logme.html loads it will access and activate the save.cgi script in the background. You might want to take out lines 64–68 in save.cgi so that the HTML from the script isn't displayed to the browser.

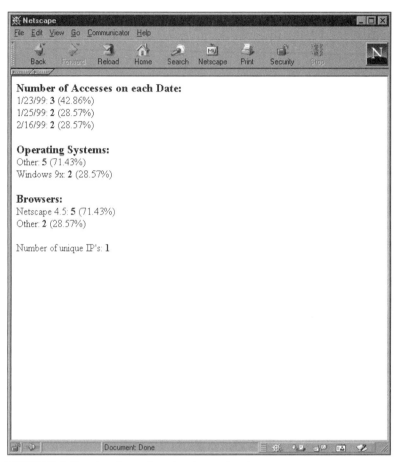

FIGURE 5–3 Results of running the view.cgi script

NOTE

Server Side Includes (SSI) are not available on all systems; they must be on a server that supports them. If this does not work, ask your system administrator if he or she can turn this on, or use a system that does allow SSI.

HTML 5–1
logme.shtml

```
<!--#exec cgi="save.cgi" -->
<HTML>
<HEAD>
<TITLE>
Log Me in Scotty!
</TITLE>
</HEAD>
<BODY>
<P>
You have been logged in...
</BODY>
</HTML>
```

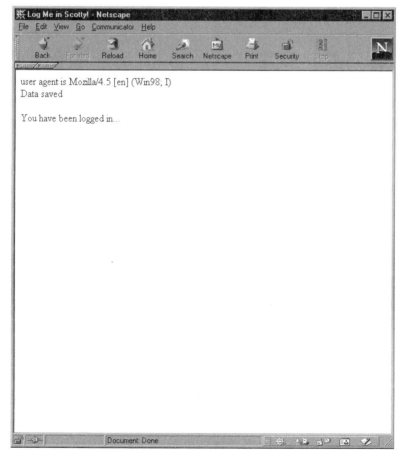

FIGURE 5–4 `<!--#exec cgi="save.cgi" -->` executes the save.cgi script to run in the background

◆ Project II: Password Protection

Files Used	Permissions
get_form_data.pl	755
read.html	644
read.cgi	755
read2.cgi	755

Sometimes you might have files that you want to protect from unwanted users, and allow only certain visitors to access with the proper username and password (or at least a shiny object). Well, since we haven't advanced to the point of sending shiny new objects to Web pages (give it a couple of years), you'll just have to learn how to password protect them.

NOTE

A more secure and preferred method is to use the password protection built into Unix known as the .htaccess file.

The following script allows a user to authenticate himself or herself and once this is done, the text document is displayed to the user. The really cool part about this is that the URL or location of the text file is never revealed! In the read.html example, the file secret1.txt is located in the same directory as read.html and read.cgi, but you can locate them anywhere as long as you give them the proper path.

This script is set up to accept three different usernames with a different password for each:

Username: user1   Password: banana
Username: user2   Password: apple
Username: user3   Password: orange

HTML 5-2
read.html

```
<HTML>
<BODY BGCOLOR="#FFFFFF">
<FORM ACTION="read.cgi" METHOD="POST">
User Name: <INPUT TYPE="TEXT" NAME="User_Name">
```

```
<BR>
Password: <INPUT TYPE="PASSWORD" NAME="Password">
<P>
<INPUT TYPE="SUBMIT" VALUE="Submit">
</FORM>
</BODY>
</HTML>
```

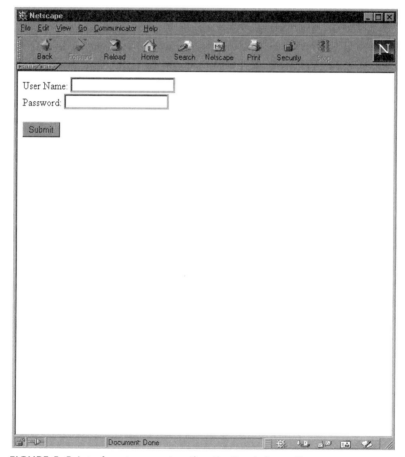

FIGURE 5–5 Interface to accept authentication information

Script 5–4
read.cgi

```
1.  #!/usr/bin/perl
2.  require "get_form_data.pl";
3.  &get_form_data;
4.  print "Content-type: text/html\n\n";
```

```
 5.  $Password{"user1"} = "banana";
 6.  $Password{"user2"} = "apple";
 7.  $Password{"user3"} = "orange";
 8.  $user = $FORM{'User_Name'};
 9.  $password = $FORM{'Password'};
10.  if(($Password{$user}) && ($password eq $Password{$user}))
11.  {
12.      $file = "secret1.txt";
13.      open(FILE, $file);
14.      while(<FILE>)
15.      {
16.          print $_;
17.      }
18.      close(FILE);
19.  }
20.  else
21.  {
22.      print <<EOF;
23.      <HTML>
24.      <BODY BGCOLOR="#FFFFFF">
25.      <B><FONT COLOR="RED">Login incorrect. Please try
         again</FONT></B>
26.      <P>
27.      <FORM ACTION="read.cgi" METHOD="POST">
28.      User Name: <INPUT TYPE="TEXT" NAME="User_Name"
         VALUE="$user">
29.      <BR>
30.      Password: <INPUT TYPE="PASSWORD" NAME="Password">
31.      <P>
32.      <INPUT TYPE="SUBMIT" VALUE="Submit">
33.      </BODY>
34.      </HTML>
35.      EOF
36.  }
```

HOW THE SCRIPT WORKS

5–7. Define passwords for three users, storing them in the associative array %Password keyed on the username.

8–9. Get the username and password the user entered in read.html.

10–19. Since $user is the username the user entered, we test to see if a password exists for that user, and if the password equals the password the user entered. If so, open secret1.txt and display its contents.

21-36. Otherwise, the username and password combination the user entered is incorrect. Provide an error page asking the user to try again.

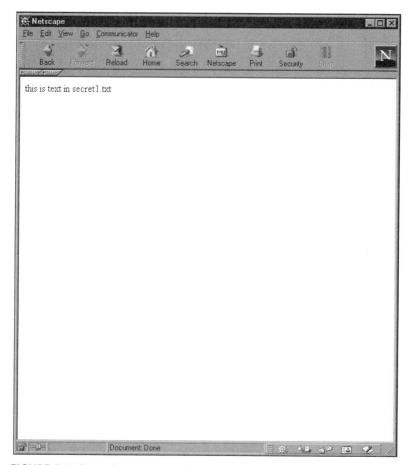

FIGURE 5-6 Once the proper authentication has been passed, the secret file is displayed

The following script is similar to the preceding one except it is slightly modified. As for the HTML, still use read.html to log in. A different file is displayed depending on which of the three users logs in.

Script 5–5
read2.cgi

```
1.  #!/usr/bin/perl
2.  require "get_form_data.pl";
3.  &get_form_data;
4.  print "Content-type: text/html\n\n";
5.  $Password{"user1"} = "banana";
6.  $Password{"user2"} = "apple";
7.  $Password{"user3"} = "orange";
8.  $File{"user1"} = "secret1.txt";
9.  $File{"user2"} = "secret2.txt";
10. $File{"user3"} = "secret3.txt";
11. $user = $FORM{'User_Name'};
12. $password = $FORM{'Password'};
13. if(($Password{$user}) && ($password eq $Password{$user}))
14. {
15.    open(FILE, $File{$user});
16.    while(<FILE>)
17.    {
18.       print $_;
19.    }
20.    close(FILE);
21. }
22. else
23. {
24.    print <<EOF;
25.    <HTML>
26.    <BODY BGCOLOR="#FFFFFF">
27.    <B><FONT COLOR="RED">Login incorrect. Please try
       again</FONT></B>
28.    <P>
29.    <FORM ACTION="read.cgi" METHOD="POST">
30.    User Name: <INPUT TYPE="TEXT" NAME="User_Name"
       VALUE="$user">
31.    <BR>
32.    Password: <INPUT TYPE="PASSWORD" NAME="Password">
33.    <P>
34.    <INPUT TYPE="SUBMIT" VALUE="Submit">
35.    </BODY>
36.    </HTML>
37.    EOF
38. }
```

HOW THE SCRIPT WORKS

5–7. Passwords are defined for three users.

8–10. A different file is associated for each of the three users.

15. This is the only other line that has changed from read.cgi. Instead of specifying `secret1.txt`, we open `$File{$user}`, since this element of `%File` contains the filename for the username the user entered.

RECAP

Environment variables are a very useful way to track users and log when and how many times a page is being visited, as well as gathering other information about them.

With read.cgi and read2.cgi you learned how to successfully navigate authenticated users to documents they would not otherwise be able to read. You can move these "secret" documents to varied places on your system that would not be viewable to the user's browser. These passwords will be valid in the examples on the companion Web site as well.

ADVANCED PROJECTS

Go back to Script 5–3, view.cgi, and modify the file so that it will have a link to a page that will show a list of all the IP addresses that have accessed the save.cgi script.

A An Introduction to Forms

One of the most powerful functions of a Web page, besides the fact that it can display information to your users, is that it can get information from them as well. This is where forms come into play, and in this appendix you will learn how to use the different forms of forms to make your forms!

Forms are just another part of HTML, but in order to make them totally useful you must incorporate them with CGI scripts; in this case, we're using Perl.

You can perform the following functions with forms:

- Get information from users and have it returned to you via e-mail, store the information into a database, or perform any number of other functions.
- Take the information retrieved from a setting file and then display the information in the fields for the user to edit.
- Have a user take a test online and evaluate his or her score immediately.
- Have a message board where users can read and post messages to and from one another.

When using forms, you always need to enclose the entire contents of the form within the <FORM> </FORM> tags so the browser treats the contents as form elements. If you do not do this, the forms will not work properly because you have to set the script location in the opening <FORM> tag.

Within the beginning <FORM> tag you need to tell this particular form what Perl script you will be using. This is done with the ACTION tag.

```
<FORM ACTION = "/cgi-bin/hello.cgi">
```

The computer isn't smart enough (yet) to figure out exactly where the script is that you want to use for this form. Therefore, using the information we discussed back in Chapter 1, you need to give the ACTION the location of your script, which will most likely be in the CGI-BIN directory at the root level of your HTML directory on the server you will be using.

Next, you need to include the METHOD of how to use the information your HTML forms are going to pass to your script. For this book we will use METHOD=POST. There is also METHOD=GET, but we will not be using that here.

```
<FORM ACTION = "/cgi-bin/hello.cgi" METHOD = "POST">
```

There you have it! You now have your form all ready to go and pointed at the correct script to use, but before you get ahead of yourself you still need to visually build the page. You can use HTML along with your forms in here. The <FORM> </FORM> tags are merely wrapping around all the HTML content so it knows to use whatever form elements are between them and handle them with the script. You can have as many forms on a Web page as you like. For example:

FORM A–1 Two separate forms with a separate text field for each. You can use one or several forms in an HTML page.

```
<HTML>
<HEAD>
<BODY BGCOLOR = "#FFFFFF">
<FORM METHOD = "POST" ACTION = "script1.cgi">
<FONT FACE = "Arial"><SMALL>
(This is script 1)</SMALL><BR>
Enter your name:</FONT><BR>
<INPUT TYPE = "text" NAME = "name" SIZE = "34"><BR>
<INPUT TYPE = "submit" VALUE = "Submit" NAME = "submit">
<INPUT TYPE = "reset" VALUE = "Reset" NAME = "submit">
</FORM>
<BR>
<FORM METHOD = "POST" ACTION = "script2.cgi">
<FONT FACE = "Arial"><SMALL>
(This is script 2)</SMALL><BR>
Enter your age:</FONT><BR>
<INPUT TYPE = "text" NAME = "name" SIZE = "5"><BR>
<INPUT TYPE = "submit" VALUE = "Submit" NAME = "submit">
<INPUT TYPE = "reset" VALUE = "Reset" NAME = "reset">
</FORM>
</BODY>
</HEAD>
</HTML>
```

With this bit of HTML, we are actually using two forms. The first one is script1.cgi, which is used to get the user's name. The second, script2.cgi, is used to get the user's age. Of course you could use the same script for both of these bits of information, this is just for demonstration purposes. For now, don't worry if you don't understand what the INPUT lines are all about, they will be explained soon enough!

All form fields allow you to pass them *attributes*. Attributes are just a simple way of telling the form fields how to behave, or sometimes to add extra functionality to the form field. Usually these are visual things like how wide or tall the particular piece will be, or if a check box or radio button has been checked or not.

The basic form elements lie within these six types of attributes:

- Submit buttons
- Single-line text box
- Text blocks
- Menus
- Check boxes
- Radio buttons

◆ Buttons

You need a way to send the information the user has just entered, and this is what the Submit button is for. Without a Submit button, users might spend half an hour entering their name, address, social security number, Swiss bank account number, and so on, before they realize that there was no way to send all this information they had just entered. This would probably prompt them to send you a nasty note thanking you for all the time they wasted.

◆ There Are Two Types of Buttons

- Submit
- Reset

```
INPUT TYPE = SUBMIT
INPUT TYPE = RESET
VALUE =   The name that visually appears on the button.
NAME =   This is the name that will be passed to the script.
```

THE SUBMIT BUTTON

```
<INPUT TYPE = "SUBMIT" VALUE = "Submit" NAME = "submit">
```

A Submit button is used to transfer all input from the fields of that form only to the CGI script that was specified in the `<FORM ACTION = "">` tag. This is a required button for every form you build; otherwise, as we mentioned earlier, users will be stuck there looking at all the valuable information they just spent hours typing in. Even worse, you won't receive any of that valuable information.

THE RESET BUTTON

```
<INPUT TYPE = "RESET" VALUE = "Reset" NAME = "reset">
```

This is for when a user wants to clear all the fields they just completed before they submit the information. This is much quicker than going back and deleting every field individually. The Reset button is not required, but it is nice to have it available for the users.

◆ Single-Line Text Box

A single-line text box is exactly what its name implies: It allows you to enter a single line of text whether it is one character, one word, or an entire sentence. You can control the visible width of the text box as well as the maximum physical length of the content that will be entered into it.

Example 1–1

FORM A–2 Single-line text box

Attributes for the single-line text box are

INPUT TYPE = "text"   This tells the browser this is a single-line text box.

NAME =   The NAME you give to this field is a unique identifier for when it passes this information to the script.

SIZE =   Sets the physical width of the box itself in characters.

MAXLENGTH =   This is the maximum number of characters that can be entered into the text box.

VALUE =   You can also set an initial value so that the text box will already have text in it. It is up to the users to delete if they wish.

Example 1–2

FORM A–3 Single-line text box with a VALUE filled in

```
<INPUT TYPE = "text" NAME = "name" SIZE = "20" MAXLENGTH
= "30" VALUE = "ENTER NAME">
```

Let's take a look at what is happening in Example 1–2.

1. The preceding code is the HTML that will make a single-line text box.
2. We assign the NAME attribute as "name".
3. The physical width of the box has been defined to 20 characters with the SIZE attribute.
4. The actual maximum amount of characters the user can type into this field is 30 as defined with MAXLENGTH.
5. An initial value is set as ENTER NAME with the VALUE attribute. If the VALUE tag is left out, then the box is displayed empty, just as in Example 1–1.

Example 2

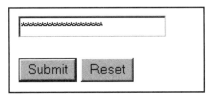

FORM A–4 Single-line text box with a VALUE filled in and the TYPE attribute set to PASSWORD instead of text. The password attribute will allow all content entered to be in asterisk format so wandering eyes don't see.

```
<input type = "password" name = "name" size = "20" VALUE
= "enter password">
```

Let's take a look at what is happening in Example 2.

1. The only difference in this example is that we're assigning the type to be password instead of text. Now everything the user types in will display only asterisks.

◆ Scrolling Text Box

The scrolling text box is similar to the single-line text box except that with the scrolling text box, you can enter several lines of text instead of just a single line. As with the single-line text box, you can set the width of the scrolling text box, but you can set the height of the box as well.

Attributes for the scrolling text box are as follows:

TEXTAREA   This tells the browser that this is a scrolling text box. Unlike all the others that start off with <INPUT TYPE="">, this will start off with <TEXTAREA>.

NAME =   The NAME you give to this field is a unique identifier for when it passes this information to the script.

ROWS =   Defines the height of the box by the amount of lines it will show before the box needs to scroll to hold additional lines.

COLS =   Defines the visual width of the box by the amount of characters the box will hold. Unlike the single-line text box, you cannot set a MAXLENGTH for the scrolling text box.

WRAP =   You can use this feature as WRAP = "virtual" so your text doesn't continue to scroll to the right until the user presses return. This will wrap the text, as the COLS limit is reached. Your users will really appreciate this.

Example 3

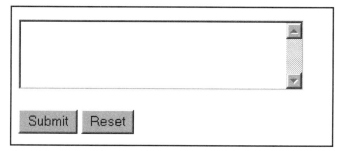

FORM A–5 Text area box, used for entering several lines

```
<TEXTAREA NAME = "information" ROWS = "4" COLS = "34"
WRAP="virtual"></TEXTAREA>
```

Let's take a look at what is happening in Example 3.

1. The preceding code is the HTML that will make a scrolling text box.
2. We assign the NAME attribute as information.
3. There will be four ROWS for height in this box.
4. The width of the box is defined with COLS as 34 characters.

As seen in the single-line text box in Example 1–2, there is a VALUE attribute where you can add predefined text to the box. You can also do this to the scrolling text box by simply adding the text between the <TEXTAREA> </TEXTAREA> tags.

Example 4

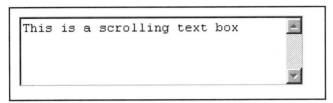

FORM A–6 Text area box with text already entered

```
<TEXTAREA NAME = "information" ROWS = "4" COLS = "34"
WRAP = "virtual">This is a scrolling text box</TEXTAREA>
```

Let's take a look at what is happening in Example 4.

1. The preceding code is the HTML that will make a scrolling text box.
2. There will be four ROWS for height in this box.
3. We assign the NAME attribute as the value "information".
4. The width of the box is defined with COLS as 34 characters.
5. The WRAP = "virtual" attribute will wrap the text as it is entered after the COLS limit is reached.
6. The content between the <TEXTAREA> and the </TEXT-AREA> tags shows that there is an initial value that the user will view. The user can leave the initial value, add to it, or simply type over it.

◆ Menus

These are sometimes known as drop-down menus because they appear as a one-line field with a little arrow to the right of it. When you point and click on the arrow, a whole menu drops down and you are presented with many options. Sometimes you are presented with too many options.

Attributes for the menus are as follows:

SELECT NAME =   The NAME you give to this field is a unique identifier for when it passes this information to the script.

SIZE =   Sets the vertical SIZE or amount of lines to show.

MULTIPLE   Allows the user to select any amount of selections you have in the menu. This is optional.

SELECTED   This is used if you would like to have an option made to be the default. This is optional.

OPTION VALUE = These are where the actual selections are made. The VALUE is like the NAME that is a unique identifier that will be passed back to the script. Between <OPTION VALUE=""> and </OPTION> is where you type in the actual text that will appear on the screen.

Example 5

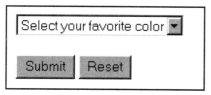

FORM A–7 The drop-down menu with just one selection showing

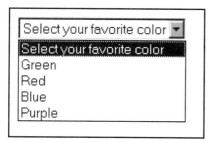

FORM A–8 The drop-down menu after the arrow has been selected to show all the possible choices the user can make

```
<SELECT NAME = "favoriteColor" SIZE="1">
<OPTION SELECTED VALUE = "Select your favorite
color ">Select your favorite color</option>
<OPTION VALUE = "Green">Green</OPTION>
<OPTION VALUE = "Red">Red</OPTION>
<OPTION VALUE = "Blue">Blue</OPTION>
<OPTION VALUE = "Purple">Purple</OPTION>
</SELECT>
```

Let's take a look at what is happening in Example 5.

1. SELECT tells the browser we want to draw a menu box.
2. NAME assigns favoriteColor as the identifier for this menu as a whole.
3. SIZE indicates that this will only be showing one line to start off with.
4. OPTION is used for each individual choice you would like to put into this menu box.

5. VALUE assigns an identifier for the choice. Don't confuse this with the NAME attribute. Think of VALUE as a sub-name for NAME.

Example 6

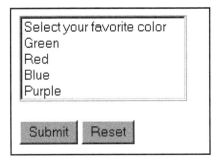

FORM A–9 The drop-down menu with the SIZE set to 5 so all five selections of the box are visible at once

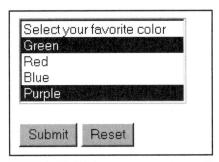

FORM A–10 With the MULTIPLE attribute set, the user can select multiple choices

```
<SELECT NAME = "favoriteColor" SIZE = "5" MULTIPLE>

    <OPTION VALUE = "Select your favorite color ">
    Select your favorite color</OPTION>
    <OPTION VALUE = "green">Green</OPTION>
    <OPTION VALUE = "red">Red</OPTION>
    <OPTION VALUE = "blue">Blue</OPTION>
    <OPTION VALUE = "purple">Purple</OPTION>
</SELECT>
```

Let's take a look at what is happening in Example 6.

This is pretty much the same as the previous example with a couple of changes to give it this particular look and feel.

1. SIZE has been changed to 5 to show all five choices in this menu. You could actually have used SIZE = 3 and showed only three lines and have a scroll bar that would scroll down to the other two choices.

2. MULTIPLE lets users select more than one choice if they wish.

◆ Check Boxes

Check boxes allow a user to select several options in a set of check boxes with the same name such as "types." The "value" is what will determine which check box was selected out of this "types" set. Suppose you want to ask users what type of music they like. Most people do not prefer just one type of music, so you want them to be able to select several types in that set of "music." To allow for this, you would simply set the NAME on all of these check boxes to be "music" and set the "value" for each to the type of music. You will see this example defined in the example HTML at the end of this appendix.

Attributes for the check box are as follows:

NAME = The NAME you give to this field is a unique identifier for when it passes this information to the script.

VALUE = This value gets sent back to the script if this box is selected and will be the output for that selection.

CHECKED If this is in the INPUT field, then this box will be CHECKED when it is drawn to the screen.

DISABLED If this is in the INPUT field, then the box will appear but the user cannot select it.

Example 7

FORM A–11 CHECKBOX—First the normal CHECKBOX, the second with attribute CHECKED to have it selected, and third the DISABLED attribute to gray the box out and make it visible but inactive

```
<input type = "checkbox" name = "checkbox_1" value = "ON">
Standard checkbox<br>
<input type = "checkbox" name = "checkbox_2" value =
"ON" checked>Checked checkbox<br>
<input type = "checkbox" name = "checkbox_3" value =
"ON" DISABLED>Disabled checkbox
```

Let's take a look at what is happening in Example 7.

1. This is a standard check box. If this is selected, then it will pass a value of ON to the variable checkbox_1 when it is passed back to the script.

2. With the CHECKED attribute added in here, the check box will automatically have itself checked and pass a value of ON to the variable checkbox_2 when it is passed back to the script.

3. This last example has the attribute DISABLED added, meaning that this is a dead box.

◆ Radio Buttons

Radio buttons are similar to check boxes in that you can have selections, but radio buttons will accept only one selection in a set. Each selection in that set will again have the same NAME and separate VALUEs just like the check box.

Attributes for the radio button are as follows:

NAME = The NAME you give to this field is a unique identifier for when it passes this information to the script.

VALUE = This value is sent back to the script if this button is selected, and will be the output for that selection.

CHECKED If this is in the INPUT field, then this button will be CHECKED when it is drawn to the screen.

DISABLED If this is in the INPUT field, then the button will appear, but the user cannot select it.

Example 8

> ⦿ Checked radio button
> ○ Unchecked radio button
> ⦾ Disabled radio button
>
> Submit | Reset

FORM A–12 RADIO BUTTON—First with the attribute CHECKED to have it selected, second an UNCHECKED radio button, and third the DISABLED attribute to make the radio button visible but inactive

```
<input type = "radio" value = "false" name = "question"
checked>Checked radio button<br>
<input type = "radio" value = "true" name = "question">
Unchecked radio button<br>
<input type = "radio" value = "true" name = "question"
DISABLED>Disabled radio button
```

Let's take a look at what is happening in Example 8.

1. With the CHECKED attribute added in here the radio button will automatically have itself checked and pass a value of FALSE to the variable question when it is sent back to the script.
2. This is a standard radio button. If this is selected, then it will pass a value of TRUE to the variable question when it is passed back to the script.
3. This last example has the attribute DISABLED added, meaning that this is basically a dead radio button.

◆ Putting It All Together

Up to this point we have covered a great deal about forms and how they work. You can have one form or several forms together on a page. The following is an example of a form you could use to gather information from users. This information could then be saved to a database file, e-mailed back to you, or used as information to build personalized pages with the information obtained from this page.

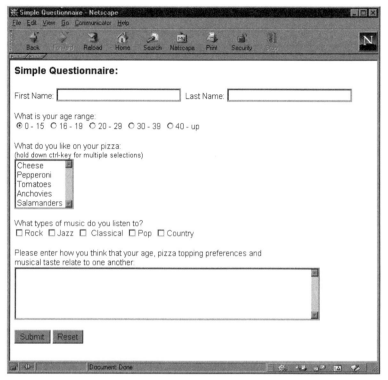

FORM A–13 Here's what several of these forms look like together on a page

```
<HTML>
<HEAD>
<TITLE>Simple Questionnaire</TITLE>

</HEAD>

<BODY BGCOLOR = "#FFFFFF">
<P><STRONG><BIG><FONT FACE = "Arial">
Simple Questionnaire:</FONT></BIG></STRONG></P>
<FORM METHOD = "POST" ACTION = "someScript.cgi">
<P>
<FONT FACE = "Arial">First Name:
<INPUT TYPE = "text" NAME = "firstName" SIZE = "20"
MAXLENGTH = "25">  Last Name:
<INPUT TYPE = "text" NAME = "lastName" SIZE = "20"></P>
<P>What is your age range:<BR>
<INPUT TYPE = "radio" VALUE = "0_15" NAME = "age"
CHECKED>0 - 15 
```

```
<INPUT TYPE = "radio" VALUE = "16_" NAME = "age">16 -
19 
<INPUT TYPE = "radio" VALUE = "20_" NAME = "age">20 -
29 
<INPUT TYPE = "radio" VALUE = "30_" NAME = "age">30 -
39 
<INPUT TYPE = "radio" VALUE = "40_above" NAME = "age">40
- up
</P>
<P>What do you like on your pizza:<BR>
<SMALL>(hold down ctrl-key for multiple selections)
</SMALL><BR>
<SELECT NAME = "toppings" SIZE = "5" MULTIPLE>
    <OPTION VALUE = "Cheese">Cheese</OPTION>
    <OPTION VALUE = "Pepperoni">Pepperoni</OPTION>
    <OPTION VALUE = "Tomatoes">Tomatoes</OPTION>
    <OPTION VALUE = "Anchovies">Anchovies</OPTION>
    <OPTION VALUE = "Salamanders">Salamanders</OPTION>
</SELECT></P>
<P>What types of music do you listen to?<BR>
<INPUT TYPE = "checkbox" NAME = "music" VALUE =
"rock">Rock 
<INPUT TYPE = "checkbox" NAME = "music" VALUE =
"jazz">Jazz 
<INPUT TYPE = "checkbox" NAME = "music" VALUE =
"classical">
Classical 
<INPUT TYPE = "checkbox" NAME = "music" VALUE =
"pop">Pop 
<INPUT TYPE = "checkbox" NAME = "music" VALUE =
"ctry">Country
</p>
<P>Please enter how you think that your age, pizza
topping preferences and<BR>
musical taste relate to one another:<BR>
<TEXTAREA ROWS = "5" NAME = "comments" COLS = "50" WRAP
= "virtual">
</TEXTAREA></P>
<P><INPUT TYPE = "submit" VALUE = "Submit" NAME =
"submit">
<INPUT TYPE = "reset" VALUE = "Reset" NAME = "reset">
</FONT></P>
</FORM>
</BODY>
</HTML>
```

B Stepping through the Perly Gates

As with every language, you must first learn how the language is constructed. With the English language we have nouns, verbs, and adjectives that make up the basic structure of the language. The same holds true for Perl with functions, statements, and operators to control how the computer reads the language.

◆ How Do I Run Perl?

Actually, if you typed in the `perl -v` command in the beginning of the book, then you have already run Perl. At that time we simply used it to get the version of Perl that you are using. Now we will use it to run Perl!

From your command line, pick an editor such as vi or pico (at a Unix prompt just type `vi` or `pico` to invoke the editor). If you are using Windows you can simply use any text editor such as Textpad or Word Pad. So, fire it up and start a file named hello.pl and enter the information in the following example.

(NOTE: Do not type in the line numbers at the left. These are line numbers we use throughout the book to explain what is happening on each of these lines in the scripts we are writing.)

Example

```
1.  #!/usr/bin/perl
2.  print "Hello yall!\n";
3.  print "I'm writing lines in Perl\n";
```

Now save the file to the directory you are going to be working in. Obviously this is a nice and simple script designed to print out two lines. To get the program to run now, type the following text at the command line:

```
perl hello.pl
```

Your screen will print back to you:

```
Hello yall!
I'm writing lines in Perl
```

1. Here we are telling the computer where to look for the Perl program. In Windows operating systems you do not need to tell the script where to look for the Perl program because it is installed as a service.
2. The `print` function prints the text in the quotes to the screen. The \n is the newline character and takes your output to the next line. The ; tells the statement that it has reached the end of the statement and to move on to the next statement.
3. Prints another line of text followed by the \n newline character.

◆ # Comments

We highly recommend using the comment tag every time you program. It is very useful for when you need to go back and look at some code that you haven't read in quite some time, or when someone else wants to eyeball your code. We can't tell you how many times we've looked at something we did even a week ago and thought "Uhmm . . . what were we doing here?" Eventually you will figure it out, but why go through all the fuss when you could just take a few seconds at the start to add some simple instructions into your code.

```
#
```

Anything after the # and on that same line will be a comment. It's really useful at the beginning of a program to put the date you started the program or write a simple little note about what the program does. You can also add comments after other text.

```
print "Hello yall!\n" # Prints Hello yall!
```

◆ Variables

Variables are names that you assign to another piece of information. They always begin with a string ($) character, which is just a dollar sign. For example, if you wanted to use the earlier program and assign `Hello yall!` and `I'm writing lines in Perl` as variables, it would look like this:

Example

```
#!/usr/bin/perl
1. $hello = "Hello yall!";
2. $text = "I'm writing lines in Perl";
3. print "$hello\n";
4. print "$text\n";
```

Output

```
Hello yall!
I'm writing lines in Perl
```

1. What we did here was assign `Hello yall` to the variable `$hello`.
2. Next we assign `I'm writing lines in Perl` to the variable `$text`.
3. Now we print out the variable `$hello`, which has the value of `Hello yall!`.
4. Finally, we print out the variable `$text`, which has the value of `I'm writing lines in Perl`.

Variables are case-sensitive, meaning upper- and lowercase need to be exact or the Perl program won't like it and will throw a temper tantrum. It is also wise to get used to a good naming convention when you name your variables. One naming scheme that we've seen most programmers stick to is to keep all the characters in lowercase, but when using a second word, capitalize the first letter in the second word. This makes it much easier to read than if you kept both words all lowercase.

Example

```
$someText = "I'm writing lines in Perl";
```

There are also two other types of variables that you can use in Perl called an *array* and an *associative array* that allow you to hold several values.

The special $_ variable

Perl has a special variable for use in many different operations, such as the current line of a loop that is reading the contents of a FILEHANDLE, or a number of regular expression matches. In the case of a loop (`while`, `foreach`, and so forth), Perl automatically copies the current line being read into $_. This can save a lot of typing time when using other operations when one or more parameters are $_. You will learn how we use $_ in the many examples in this book.

◆ Arrays

An array is a special type of variable that contains multiple scalar values. The array is an ordered list of these values; they have a set sequence from the first element to the last.

```
@users = ("Chris", "Micah", "Dan");
```

Here, we define the `@users` array as containing three elements, `Chris`, `Micah`, and `Dan`. All arrays are referenced using `@`, and individual elements in the array are referenced using `$`, just like regular scalar variables. In this case, the preceding command would be the same as doing:

```
$users[0] = "Chris";
$users[1] = "Micah";
$users[2] = "Dan";
```

Now, to access these elements, we simply reference the array with its numeric subscript.

```
print "The second user is $users[1]\n";
```

The subscript of an element of an array can also be specified by another variable.

```
$num = 2;
print "The third user is $users[$num]\n";
```

Rapid traversing of all elements in an array can be done by using `while`/`for` loops, substituting the subscript with the counter variable from the loop.

Associative Arrays

An associative array (also called a *hash*) is a lot like a normal array in that it is a collection of scalar values each selected by some index value. The difference is that this index value can be any scalar, not just an integer. These scalars are called *keys* and are used to call the values from the array.

The individual elements of an associative array are not arranged in any particular order. Perl stores the values in its own internal order, which makes it easier for Perl to find the matching value without examining every single element.

Remember that we refer to an array with @; with associative arrays, we refer to them with % instead. Just like regular arrays, however, when accessing individual elements we use $, only instead of using square brackets ([]), we use curly ones ({}). The key, which was mentioned earlier, appears between the brackets. This key can either be explicitly declared, or we can use a variable to represent it.

◆ Whitespace

When using `print` functions, any extra whitespace between the quotes, whether single or double, will be printed. This also holds true for tabs and spaces.

Example

```
1. print "It hurts to stare at the sun\n";
2. print "It    hurts    to    stare    at    the    sun\n";
3. print "It hurts to stare at the        sun\n";
```

Output

```
1. It hurts to stare at the sun
2. It    hurts    to    stare    at    the    sun
3. It hurts to stare at the        sun
```

1. This line is printed using single spaces between the words ending with a \n newline character.
2. We use triple spaces between each of the words, and as you can see, they are all printed to the screen.
3. Toward the end there is a tab between the and sun, which is also printed to the screen.

When we assign a value to a variable we can use whitespace rather randomly to make things a little easier to read.

```
   Example#!/usr/bin/perl
1. $number = 5;
2. $firstName = "Micah";
3. $lastName
4. =
5. "Brown"
6. ;
7. print "$firstName $lastName is $number years old\n\n";
```

1. There is no space in this line, and the value of $number is 5.
2. We put a space before and after the = to make it a little easier to read, but the value of $firstName is Micah with no space added at the beginning before Micah.
3. Lines 3–6 are the equivalent of writing this statement all on one line. We have just taken each part of this statement and put it on its own line. The program knows it has reached the end of the statement when it encounters the semicolon (;) on line 6.

Output

```
Micah Brown is 5 years old
```

◆ Errors

Before we go much further, you should know that no matter how hard you try, you will still run into errors when you run your Perl programs—there's just no way around it. However, one thing that's really nice about Perl is that it helps you out when you need it, for the most part anyway. When you go to run the program, Perl will step through the program and report any errors it finds. What it reports back to you doesn't always make the most sense, but you can usually track down a few errors. The majority of the time you are simply missing a quotation mark, an operator, or you have mistyped something. Usually, if there are several errors, most of them are caused by the first error. It's the domino effect. It's a good idea to fix the first problem, then run the program again to see if any of the other errors come up.

◆ Functions

Print

The first function we will discuss is `print`, which is used to print output to the screen. Pretty simple, eh? You will use `print` to pass one or more arguments or parameters through your program. Here are a couple of examples:

```
print "Hello yall!";
print $hello;
```

Print will pass the information to the right of the `print` function to the screen. Now, you might be wondering why we're using quotes in the first line and not in the second. Don't despair, we will be covering this in the next page or two.

Chop

What the `chop()` function does is `chop` off the last character from a line of text. For example:

```
$text = "This is a great book";
chop ($text);
```

This would produce the value of `$text` with the last character chopped off:

```
This is a great boo
```

OK, so this isn't particularly useful in this case, right? It will become very useful in the future when you learn to use `<STDIN>`, and the newline character is appended to the end of the text.

If you were to have the following line in your script:

```
$text = <STDIN>;
```

and the user were to type *"This is a great book,"* you would end up with this:

```
$text = "This is a great book\n";
```

The `chop` function will strip off that nasty `\n` and leave you with "This is a great book" without the newline character.

```
$text = "This is a great book";
```

Reading Input

<STDIN>

You are probably looking at the example we put in the chop function and wondering what the <STDIN> was all about, right? This stands for **ST**an**D**ard **IN**put, which Perl uses to grab what you've typed and assign it to a variable. As mentioned before, a newline \n character will be added to the end of what was typed in.

In the following example we will use <STDIN> to grab your first and last name and assign them to the variables $firstname and $lastname and display them:

```perl
#!/usr/bin/perl
1.  print "Enter your first name: ";
2.  $firstName = <STDIN>;
3.  chop($firstName);

4.  print "Enter your last name: ";
5.  $lastName = <STDIN>;
6.  chop($lastName);
7.  print "\n\nYour full name is: $firstName $lastName\n\n";
```

Output

```
Your full name is: Micah Brown
```

1. You are prompted to enter your first name.
2. <STDIN> takes what you have entered, in this case Micah, and assigns it to the variable $firstName.
3. The chop command gets rid of the newline character that was added to the variable when <STDIN> was invoked.
4. You are prompted for your last name.
5. <STDIN> takes what you have entered, in this case Brown, and assigns it to the variable $lastName.
6. Again the chop command gets rid of the newline character.
7. The program prints two newline characters with \n\n to the screen, then tells us our full name with what is stored in $firstName and $lastName.

◆ Quotes

As you might have noted earlier in this chapter, we used single quotes (' ') and double quotes (" ") in different places. There are reasons for using each. You can put a value of a string in either single quotes (' ') or double quotes (" ") and assign it to a variable.

```perl
#!/usr/bin/perl

$singleQuotes = '5';
$doubleQuotes = "5";

print "$singleQuotes\n";
print "$doubleQuotes\n";
```

Output

```
5
5
```

The difference is that when it comes to printing out a variable you need to have it within double quotes or you will get an unexpected result. If you take the preceding program and use single quotes on lines 3 and 4, here is what would happen:

```perl
#!/usr/bin/perl

$singleQuotes = '5';
$doubleQuotes = "5";

print '$singleQuotes\n';
print '$doubleQuotes\n';
```

Output

```
$singleQuotes\n$doubleQuotes\n
```

As you can see, this is not exactly what we wanted. If you want to print out the contents of a variable you need to use double quotes. This also holds true when you want to use an escape character, such as the \n character.

◆ open

The open function allows you to open a file to read, write, or append to. You can also use this to open a process such as sendmail through a pipe (|).

Syntax

Opening a file:

```
open(FILEHANDLE, "FILENAME") ;
```

Opening a process:

```
open(FILEHANDLE, "|/usr/sbin/sendmail");
```

◆ FILEHANDLES

FILEHANDLES are used as unique identifiers, or labels, when accessing other files when opening, closing, editing, or doing anything with that file. They are also usually named in uppercase, although this is not necessary, as they will work in lowercase. As a proper rule you should name them in uppercase.

Syntax

```
open(ARTICLE1, ">article1.txt");
```

When referring to article1.txt you will use the `ARTICLE1` as the FILEHANDLE.

Syntax

```
print ARTICLE1 "this will be added to article1.txt";
```

NOTE

You can give FILEHANDLEs any name you wish, other than those used by the Perl language.

◆ close

Whenever you open a file or a process, it is usually good practice to close it when you are finished using it. This is not required, but not doing so can produce some problems.

Syntax

Closing a file:

```
open(FILEHANDLE, "FILENAME") ;
close(FILEHANDLE);
```

Closing a process:

```
open(FILEHANDLE, "|/usr/sbin/sendmail");
close(FILEHANDLE);
```

opendir

```
opendir(FILEHANDLE, "directory");
```

Similar to the `open` function where you specify a FILEHANDLE for a folder instead of a file to be opened.

closedir

```
closedir(FILEHANDLE);
```

Just like the `open` function had to be closed, now the `opendir` function must be closed.

◆ readdir

The `readdir` function gives us a list of all the files and directories contained in the FILEHANDLE specified. When used in a scalar context, `readdir` returns the next filename. When using `readdir` in an array context, all remaining files and directories are placed into an array as a list with one name per element. Also, the order that files and directories are given corresponds exactly to the order in which the filesystem stores the files and directories. Here are some examples:

```
opendir(DIR, ".");
foreach $name (readdir(DIR))
{
    print "$name\n";
}
closedir(DIR);
```

This prints out every file and directory residing in the current directory (.). We can also use the `sort` command to display the names sorted alphabetically; simply replace the second line with:

```
foreach $name (sort readdir(DIR))
```

Also, we can put the contents of a directory into an array like this:

```
@files = sort readdir(DIR);
```

◆ Opening Other Programs

Using the `open` command, you can open files, directories, or even other programs. To open the sendmail program, the syntax would be

```
open(FILEHANDLE, "|/usr/sbin/sendmail")
```

| is the pipe command that allows you to use another program such as sendmail. If you wish to open another program, simply substitute the path of sendmail with the path of the other program.

◆ flock

`flock` is used to lock a file so that nothing else can write to it while it is locked except the script that locked it.

```
flock(FILEHANDLE, "FILE_LOCKING_NAME");
```

Name	Operation	Function
Lock_sh	1	Creates a shared lock
Lock_ex	2	Creates an exclusive lock
Lock_nb	4	Creates a nonblocking lock
Lock_un	8	Unlocks an existing lock

Example

```
$lock_ex = 2;
$lock_un = 8;
open(FILEHANDLE, ">>file.txt");
1. flock(FILEHANDLE, "$lock_ex");
print "FILEHANDLE, "something";
2. flock "(FILEHANDLE, "$lock_un";
```

1. `$lock_ex` locks the FILEHANDLE with an exclusive lock which only the script that created this lock has access to.
2. `$lock_un` now unlocks the FILEHANDLE so that others can write to the file.

◆ push

The push command simply adds a scalar value to the end of an array:

```
push(@thisarray, $somevalue);
```

So, if the elements of @thisarray were (1, 2, 3, 4), then after executing this line @thisarray would contain (1, 2, 3, 4, $somevalue).

◆ pop

The pop command does the opposite of push: It removes the last element of an array and returns it.

```
$lastelement = pop(@thisarray);
```

◆ Operators

Operator	Description	Order of Precedence
++	Auto-increment	Not applicable
--	Auto-decrement	Not applicable
**	Exponentiation	Right-to-Left
=~, !~	Pattern matching	Left-to-Right
+	Addition	Left-to-Right
−	Subtraction	Left-to-Right
.	Concatenation	Left-to-Right
*	Multiplication	Left-to-Right
/	Division	Left-to-Right
%	Modulation (remainder)	Left-to-Right
<<, >>	Shifting operators	Left-to-Right
&	Bitwise and	Left-to-Right
|	Bitwise or	Left-to-Right
||	Logical or	Left-to-Right
&&	Logical and	Left-to-Right
..	List range operator	Left-to-Right
,	Comma Separator	Left-to-Right
? and :	Conditional operator (together)	Right-to-Left

Comparative Operators

NUMERIC

Comparative operators are used to evaluate whether integers you will be testing are true or false.

Numeric Operator	Description	Order of Precedence
<	Less than	Left-to-Right
>	Greater than	Left-to-Right
==	Equal to	Left-to-Right
<=	Less than or equal to	Left-to-Right
>=	Greater than or equal to	Left-to-Right
!=	Not Equal to	Left-to-Right
<=>	Comparison returning –1, 0, or 1	Left-to-Right

Here are a few examples to help you understand how each of these work:

$num < 50   True if $num has a value lower than 50. If $num has a value of 50 or above, then it is false.

$num > 50   True if $num has a value higher than 50. If $num has a value of 50 or below, then it is false.

$num == 50   True if $num has a value of 50. If $num has a value other than 50, then it is false.

$num <= 50   True if $num has a value lower than 50 or is equal to 50. If $num has a value of 51 or above, then it is false.

$num >= 50   True if $num has a value higher than 50 or is equal to 50. If $num has a value of 49 or below, then it is false.

$num != 50   True if $num is not equal to 50. If $num has the value of anything other than 50, then it is false.

$num <=> 50   This operator is different from the others. This will evaluate to 0 if $num and 50 are equal. If $num is less than 50, then it will be evaluated to 1. If $num is more than 50, it will be evaluated to –1.

String Comparison Operator

String comparison operators are another way to compare the value of string. String values are in alphabetical order; for example, aaa comes before bbb.

String Operator	Description	Numeric Equivalent
lt	Less than	<
gt	Greater than	>
eq	Equal to	==
le	Less than or equal to	<=
ge	Greater than or equal to	>=
ne	Not equal to	!=
cmp	Comparison returning –1, 0 or 1	<=>

Here are a few examples:

`$text = "aaa" lt "bbb";`   True because aaa comes before bbb.

`$text = "aaa" gt "bbb";`   False because aaa is not greater than bbb.

`$text = "aaa" eq "bbb";`   False because aaa and bbb are not equal.

`$text = "aaa" le "bbb";`   True because aaa is less than bbb.

`$text = "aaa" ge "bbb";`   False because aaa is not greater than or equal to bbb.

`$text = "aaa" ne "bbb";`   True because aaa and bbb are not equal values.

`$text = "aaa" cmp "bbb";`   Result is 1 because the second value (bbb) is greater than the first value (aaa).

◆ Escape Sequences

These are sequences of characters that consist of a backslash (\) followed by one or more characters that perform certain duties. The most common one you will see is \n, which will format a new

line. When you use the backslash, the next character following it
will perform some action. If you would like to actually print the
character \, then you would simply throw a \ in front of that: \\.

Escape Sequence	Description
\a	Bell or a beep
\b	Backspace
\e	Escape
\f	Form feed
\l	Force next character into lowercase
\L	Force all following characters into lowercase
\n	Newline
\r	Carriage return
\t	Tab
\u	Force the next character into uppercase
\U	Force all following characters into uppercase
\v	Vertical tab

Example

```
1.  #!/usr/bin/perl

2.  # This will print a receipt for a horse and saddle
3.  $horse = 250;
4.  $saddle = 5;
5.  $total = ($horse + $saddle);

6.  print "Hello, please tell me your name: ";
7.  $name = <>;
8.  chop $name;

9.  print "$name, here is your bill:\n";
10. print "Horse:\t \$ $horse \n";
11. print "Saddle:\t \$ $saddle\n";
12. print "TOTAL:\t \$ $total\n\n";
```

Output

```
Hello, please tell me your name: Micah
Micah, here is your bill:
Horse:   $ 250
Saddle: $ 5
TOTAL:   $ 255
```

We will use the program in the preceding example to discuss what we have covered so far in this appendix. Now, you might be thinking, "Wow! This is a good deal on a horse and saddle!" If this is the case, then we're sorry. We don't know where to find a deal like this.

If you don't understand a few of these right away, don't be discouraged, simply go back and read up on it again.

1. Tells the computer where to find the Perl program to execute the script.
2. Comments to describe what the script is going to do.
3. Sets the value of 250 to the variable $horse.
4. Sets the value of 5 to the variable $saddle.
5. Sets the value of the variable $total to what $horse and $saddle are once they are added together.
6. Prints the line: Hello, please tell me your name: to the screen. This is the first line in the script that will be displayed to the user.
7. Here the program halts and awaits input from the user. Once the user enters a name and presses return, the input is then assigned to the variable $name.
8. Removes the newline that was automatically added from the end of the $name string.
9. The name that the user from line 8 entered will be displayed here with $name followed by the rest of the sentence, then followed by the \n character, which will bring you to the next line.
10. Prints Horse:, then the \t will print a tab after that. We then have the \$ character, which will print a $, and then is followed by the variable $horse, which was given the value of 250 back on line 4.
11. Prints Saddle:, then the \t will print a tab after that. We then have the \$ character, which will print a $, and then is followed by the variable $saddle, which was given the value of 5 back on line 5.
12. Finally, we print TOTAL:, then the \t will print a tab after that. We then have the \$ character, which will print a $ and then is followed by the variable $total, which back in line 6 was given the value of $horse and $saddle, which were 250 and 5, respectively.

printf

The printf operator is used for printing out formatted text. It takes a list of arguments just like print. The first argument is a format control string, which defines how to print out the remaining arguments. Following this control string are the variable(s) that will be printed out. Consider the following example:

```
printf "%5s %5.2f %15d", $a, $b, $c;
```

This line prints out $a as a 5-character field (the s after the 5 stands for string), followed by a space, then $b as a floating point value with 2 decimal places in a 5-character field, then another space, followed by $c as a 15-character decimal integer.

◆ Jumping through Loops

Loops are a great way to do something repeatedly a certain amount of times with a relatively small amount of code. Everything we've done up until now has been pretty straightforward: The script executes from top to bottom without the need to branch off into other parts of the script. What we have done up until now is known as *unconditional statements*, since there are no conditions being set on the code.

With loops, however, we can have the script execute certain statements based upon when certain conditions are met. For example, if your script asks, "How many pennies are there in a dollar?" and the user enters 100, you can have the script answer "Very good, you get a gold star." If the user enters 5, you can have the script execute another set of instructions to say, "Please try again."

Depending on what you are doing in your scripts will determine the best time to use loops. They are a very important part of Perl, as well as any programming language, but we promise we will try to explain them as painlessly as possible.

For example, remember when you were a kid and you would get into an argument with the kid next door over who put a dent in your mother's car. It would go something like this:

"You put the dent in the car!"

"Did not! ... Did too! ... Did not! ... Did too! ..."

And this would go on for, say, 50 more times until one of you just gave in, or the two of you got bored. Well, basically, that is a loop, and there is a much simpler way to do that instead of wasting all of your valuable time bickering back and forth so you could go out and get into more trouble.

while loop

With the `while` statement, we take a variable that has earlier been assigned a value and test it to see whether it is true or not. This is called the *condition*. If the condition of the variable is true, then the statement will be executed. If the condition of the variable is found to be false, then the statement after the `while` will be ignored and we move on to the next part of the code.

```
while  (condition)
{
    ( statement );
}
```

We will start off using the `while` loop to complete this meaningful exchange of words.

```
#!/usr/bin/perl
1. print "You put a dent in the car!\n";
2. while ($num < 50)
3. {
4.     print "Did not!\t";
5.     print "Did too!\n";
6.     $num++;
7. }
8. print "I win! nyah nyah!\n\n";
```

Output

```
You put a dent in the car!
Did not!        Did too!
Did not!        Did too!
Did not!        Did too!
```

......47 more times...

```
I win! nyah nyah!
```

This seems like a much easier solution than to have

```
print "Did not!\t Did too\n";
```

50 times, correct? Let's take a look at the code and determine exactly what is happening.

1. Prints `You put a dent in the car` to the screen followed by the `\n` newline character.

2. Here we start the `while` conditional loop by telling it that while the value of `$num` (which currently has no value assigned to it) is less than 50 (which it is), to do the next statement.

3. Since we are going to be using more than just one statement after the `while` loop, we need to block these lines off so that Perl knows to execute the statements within these brackets `{}` collectively. This is the beginning of what's called a *block statement*.

4. During the `while` statement, this is the first line that is printed.

5. Still in the `while` statement, this second line is now printed.

6. Now the value of `$num` is incremented by 1 and the value now is 1.

7. The ending bracket `}` tells Perl that this is the end of this block statement.

8. Finally, we print out a childish response, letting the other person know he has been defeated in this loop!

for loop

Using the `for` statement, we can initially set the variable we would like to use directly in the `for` statement if it hasn't already been set beforehand.

```
for    ( set variable; condition; update variable )
{
    ( statement );
}
```

If we have set the variable beforehand and won't be dealing with it, then we still need to set the semicolon. Once we set the variable (`$num = 0`) we can test the condition of it for this statement. So, we would like to see if `$num` is less than 50. If this is TRUE, then increment `$num` by 1 and do the statement after the `for` statement and test this again. When `$num` finally goes through several times and gets incremented up to 50, then the `for` statement is finished and the script can move on.

```
   #!/usr/bin/perl
1. for ($num = 0; $num < 50; $num++)
2. {
3.    print "Did too!\t";
4.    print "Did not!\n";
5. }
6. print "I win! nyah nyah!\n\n";
```

Output

```
You put a dent in the car!
Did not!        Did too!
Did not!        Did too!
Did not!        Did too!
```

...47 more times...

```
I win! nyah nyah!
```

You might be looking at this and thinking, "This is much simpler, and there's less to type, so why don't we just do this all the time instead of using the while loop?" Well, there is one important difference with the for loop that the while loop can't do. If the value of $num were already set to 50 from earlier in the script, then when we get to the conditional part of the for loop (which tests if $num is less than 50), it will evaluate it as being false. So, if it is false, there is no reason to execute the block statement on line 25, so it will go directly to line 6.

1. We assign a new variable called $num and give it the value of 0. Next we test the variable to see if it is less than 50; since this is true, we then print the block statement on lines 2–5 and increment it by 1.
2. Start of the block statement.
3. Prints the first line of the block statement.
4. Prints the second line of the block statement.
5. Ends the block statement.
6. Finally, we print out the childish response letting the other person know that he has been defeated in this loop!

On line 1, when $num is assigned the value of 0, $num is checked to see if it is less than 50. If it is not (meaning true), it then goes ahead and prints out the statements in the statement block on lines 2 and 3 before it is incremented to 1, even though $num++ comes right after this. After this is done, $num then gets the increment $num++.

◆ If Statement

```
if ( expression )
    ( statement );
```

The `if` statement is also known as a conditional statement and is the most basic conditional statement that you will use with Perl. It simply evaluates whether or not an expression is true or false. If the expression is evaluated as true, then the `if` will go to the statement directly after it; otherwise, if it is evaluated as false, then the `if` statement is finished and will move on without printing its statement. You can also use statement blocks with the `if` statement to have multiple statements if the expression is true.

```
if ( expression )
{
    ( statement 1 );
    ( statement 2 );
    ( statement 3 );
}
```

◆ foreach

The `foreach` function is another one of the looping functions. This is used when sorting through an array, where it will start with the first element in the array and perform whatever statement it has after it on the element. When finished with the statements, the second element in the array will be selected and the process begins again until all elements in the array have been looped through.

```
#!/usr/bin/perl
@count = ('1', '2', '3', '4', '5');
print "I can count to: \n";
foreach $count (@count)
{
    print $count, "\n";
}
```

Results

```
I can count to:
1
2
3
4
5
```

◆ local

Up to now, the variables you have used have been global through-out the entire program. However, sometimes when using these variables you would like to make a variable's value only valid for a certain subroutine, then once the subroutine is exited, return back to its old value.

```perl
#!/usr/bin/perl
$number = 5;
print "\$number is equal to: $number\n";
&new_routine;
sub new_routine
{
    local ($number);
    $number = 10;
    print "Inside local, \$number is equal to: $number\n";
}
print "\$number is now equal to: $number\n\n";
```

Results

```
$number is equal to: 5
Inside local, $number is equal to: 10
$number is now equal to: 5
```

◆ Regular Expressions

Regular expressions are a powerful tool used in Perl. A regular expression is a pattern to be matched against any string. Matching a regular expression against a string either succeeds or fails. Usually, this success or failure is all the script cares about. Other times, you may want to replace a certain string with another string like a search and replace. In Perl, regular expressions are expressed by sur-rounding the string to be matched in forward slashes.

```perl
if(/something/)
{
    print "we found something in $_\n";
}
```

You may ask, "What are we testing the regular expression against?" Here is where the special $_ variable comes into play. When a target is not specified (more on how to specify a target later), any regular expression is performed on $_. In this example, if $_ contains the string something, then it is printed out that it has been found.

What if you want to replace a certain string with another string? Instead of just putting slashes around our regular expression, the letter s (substitution) is inserted in front of the first slash, followed by the pattern to be matched, then another slash to separate the two, then the pattern with which to replace the first pattern, and finally, another slash.

```
s/something/something else/g;
```

This line replaces the string something with something else in $_.

NOTE

The =~ character tests to see if both sides are true, like you used == earlier, only =~ is used to test regular expressions.

! = does the exact opposite by testing to see if both sides are not equal to each other. If they are not, then this will result in true.

What if you want to perform a regular expression search and replace on a variable other than $__? This is where the =~ operator is used. Just as before, you may only be interested in whether or not the regular expression succeeded. Either way, the syntax for the regular expression is the same, you will just use it like this:

```
if($something =~ /something/)
{
    print "we found something \n";
}
```

If $something contains the text something, again, it is simply printed out that it has been found.

```
$something =~ s/something/something else/;
```

Now replace any and all occurrences of something with something else in $something.

◆ localtime

The `localtime` function returns an array of nine elements of time in the following order:

```
($sec,$min,$hour,$mday,$mon,$year,$wday,$yday,$isdst) =
localtime(time);
```

Array Number	Value
0	Seconds
1	Minutes
2	Hour of the day (0–23)
3	Day of the Month
4	Month (0=January, 11=December)
5	Year (with 1900 subtracted from it)
6	Day of the Week (0-Sunday, 6=Saturday)
7	Day of the Year (0–364)
8	A flag indicating whether it is daylight savings time

◆ File Permissions

With Unix you will need to give certain types of permission to files or programs when you plan to use them in certain situations. This is used for security reasons so others won't be able to access your files when you don't want them to; however, there are ways to let them do this if you so choose. To get a listing of your files in long file format and to see the permissions associated with it, go to your Unix prompt and type:

```
ls -l
```

Output

```
-rwxrwxrwx   1 users     micah        0 Nov  1 13:22
email.cgi

-rwxrwxrwx
         └──────── World ( O - other )
       └────────── Group ( G - group )
     └──────────── Owner ( U - user )
```

There are three types of levels associated with your files or programs:

- Owner (U-user)   This is the person who owns the file. In this case, it happens to be Micah.
- Group (G-group)   This is the group that the owner belongs to, which is *users*.
- World (O-other)   This is everyone else outside the group.

Each of these has three levels associated with them as well:

Privilege (Rights)	Letter Value
r–Read	r
w–Write	w
x –Execute	x

To change the rights that a file has you will need to assign it a letter value with the chmod (change mode) function. For example, if you would like to change the rights for the file email.cgi so group has execute rights, you would type:

```
chmod g+x email.cgi
```

Here you are telling the file email.cgi to change the level of group to have the privilege of execute. Now anyone in your group may go in and execute this file. If you wish to reverse this and not let group has this privilege, then you simply type:

```
chmod g-x email.cgi
```

This will take the execution privilege away from group and they will no longer be able to execute email.cgi.

The chmod command works the same for all three levels of owner, group, and world. Here's a list of all the modes you can change on your files.

Users (read, write, execute)
```
chmod u+r email.cgi
chmod u+w email.cgi
chmod u+x email.cgi
```

Group (read, write, execute)
```
chmod g+r email.cgi
chmod g+w email.cgi
chmod g+x email.cgi
```

Others (read, write, execute)

```
chmod o+r email.cgi
chmod o+w email.cgi
chmod o+x email.cgi
```

You may even combine the levels and permissions to change multiple permission on a file at once.

```
chmod ugo+rwx email.cgi
```

This will give owner, group, and world the read, write, and execute privileges to the email.cgi file.

◆ Subroutines

Just as Perl has its own internal system functions, you, too, can define your own. A user function, also called a *subroutine*, or just a *sub*, is defined as follows:

```
sub sub_name
{
    statement 1;
    statement 2;
    statement 3;
}
```

The block of statements after the name of the subroutine constitutes the definition of the subroutine. When the subroutine is called, the block of statements defined by the subroutine is executed, and any return value is returned to the caller.

As an example, here is a subroutine that prints the famous phrase:

```
sub hello_world
{
    print "Hello World\n";
}
```

Remember from Chapter 1 that we can call a subroutine from anywhere in the program, even another subroutine (or the subroutine itself). Subroutine definitions can also appear anywhere in the program, and the order of the subroutine blocks is inconsequential to the order in which they are called. Subroutines are read and defined before anything gets executed, so a subroutine call can be placed above the actual definition. For this reason, many prefer to put their subroutines at the bottom of the file so that the main part of the program appears at the beginning of the file.

To call the function, precede the subroutine name with an ampersand:

```
&hello_world;
```

User-defined functions can also have *return* values. Return values consist of one or more values returned to a variable or array assigned to the subroutine call. For example, consider the following:

```
sub add_two_numbers
{
    $a + $b;
}
```

Now, to call this function, we simply assign it to a variable.

```
$a = 4;
$b = 5;
$c = &add_two_numbers;
```

Similarly, we can return a list of values and store them in an array.

```
sub list_of_two_numbers
{
    ($a,$b);
}
    $a = 10;
$b = 20;
@c = &list_of_two_numbers;
```

@c now contains (10, 20).

Functions can also pass *arguments*. If we call the function, as before, using an ampersand and the function name, followed by a list of values separated by commas in parentheses, we can act upon whatever those values passed are. When a value is passed to a function, Perl assigns the list of these values to the special array.

```
sub sum_of
{
    $_[0] + $_[1];
}
```

```
$sum = &sum_of(5,10);
$sum2 = &sum_of(2,8);
```

In the first line after the function definition, the values of 5 and 10 are passed to the &sum_of function, and using the special @_ variable, they are added together. This resulting value is then assigned into the $sum variable. The same thing goes for the second line. Excess values are passed to a function, but those never used are simply ignored, and undefined elements of the @_ array simply contain the value undef.

◆ require

The require function is used to call another Perl script to use routines that are included within that file. This is a great way to modularize your scripts. Throughout the book, the form parsing routine will be placed on its own in a file called get_form_data.pl, so it can be called at the beginning of each script without actually existing within that script, thus saving you from rewriting it into each script. Another benefit of this is that if you were to make a change to get_form _data.pl, the change would be updated throughout each script, whereas, if you were to have this routine in each script, you would have to change it for each one.

Additionally, you can hold several subroutines within a separate file and call the routine you need. You can even have several subroutines within this document that one file calls but another does not. If it isn't called, it simply isn't used.

Syntax

```
require "get_form_data.pl";
```

C Miscellaneous Reference

◆ Reasons Why Your Scripts May Not Be Working Properly

- Permissions are not set properly.
- File or files are uploaded in binary format instead of ASCII.
- Perl location is not set properly (`#!/usr/bin/perl`).
- Wrong path is set in the HTML document.
- Perl doesn't exist on the machine on which you are running the script, or it's an old version.
- There is a typo in the script: Try running the script from the command line to detect and fix errors.
- Required files are missing.

◆ Resources

Mailing Lists

PERL FAQ A DAY

http://www.yoak.com/daily_perl
Perl FAQ a Day is a one-way mailing list that delivers a randomly selected question/answer pair from *The PERL FAQ* to you daily.

Web Sites

FREE PERL CODE

http://www.FreePerlCode.com
Various Perl code examples of several types of applications.

PERL WEB RING

http://www.netaxs.com/~joc/perlring.html
http://www.webring.org/cgi-bin/webring?ring=perl;list
A Web ring consisting of about 100 Perl-oriented Web sites linked together with everything from snippets of code to tutorials to full-blown scripts for you to use.

Newsgroups

alt.perl
comp.lang.perl.misc
comp.lang.perl.moderated
comp.lang.perl.modules

Programs Worth Checking Out

TEXT EDITOR

Windows

www.allaire.com
HomeSite 4.0
Allaire HomeSite 4.0 is the award-winning HTML editing tool that lets you build great Web sites in less time while maintaining pure HTML. The intuitive HomeSite WYSIWYN (what you see is what you need) interface puts the tools you need right at your fingertips.

Mac

http:web/barebones.com/
BBEdit
BBEdit is the premier text and HTML editor for the MacOS. It has long been regarded as the staple editing tool for both HTML and software development. BBEdit is highly extensible. Users benefit from BBEdit's plug-in architecture whether using existing third-party plug-ins or writing their own. The feature list is enormous (and includes things like syntax coloring for Perl)—for a more detailed description, visit the Bare Bones Software Web site.

Perl

ActivePerl

ActivePerl is the latest Perl binary distribution from ActiveState and replaces what was previously distributed as Perl for Win32. The latest release of ActivePerl, as well as other Perl-related tools, are available from the ActiveState Web site at http://www.ActiveState.com.

ActiveState, ActivePerl, PerlScript, and Perl for Win32 are trademarks of ActiveState Tool Corp.

Index

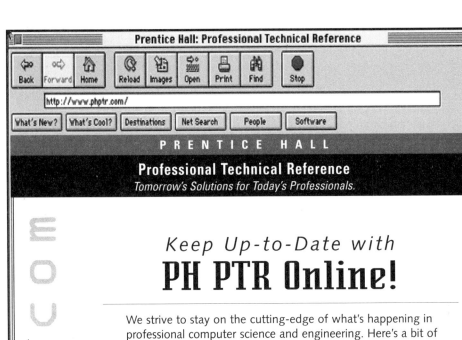